LEONARD COHEN

For Dylan Lev, welcome to the world

LEONARD COHEN

The Mystical Roots of Genius

Harry Freedman

BLOOMSBURY CONTINUUM
LONDON • OXFORD • NEW YORK • NEW DELHI • SYDNEY

BLOOMSBURY CONTINUUM
Bloomsbury Publishing Plc
50 Bedford Square, London, WC1B 3DP, UK
29 Earlsfort Terrace, Dublin 2, Ireland

First published in Great Britain 2021
Paperback 2024

A catalogue record for this book is available from the British Library

Library of Congress Cataloguing-in-Publication data has been applied for

ISBN: PB: 978-1-3994-1649-8; eBook: 978-1-4729-8728-0;
ePDF: 978-1-4729-8726-6

2 4 6 8 10 9 7 5 3 1

Typeset by Deanta Global Publishing Services, Chennai, India
Printed and bound in Great Britain by CPI Group (UK) Ltd, Croydon CR0 4YY

To find out more about our authors and books visit www.bloomsbury.com
and sign up for our newsletters

Praise for *Leonard Cohen: The Mystical Roots of Genius*

'Leonard Cohen taught us that even in the midst of darkness there is light, in the midst of hatred there is love, with our dying breath we can still sing Hallelujah.'

Rabbi Jonathan Sacks

'Freedman's book highlights even further layers of meaning to the songs which speak so profoundly to so many of us, regardless of faith or spiritual background.'

The National Herald (US)

'For those who know and want to know even more, this account of Leonard Cohen's preoccupations and what he made from his knowledge of the religious, is fascinating. A cultural story of a cultural giant.'

Susie Orbach, psychotherapist and author

'*Leonard Cohen: The Mystical Roots of Genius* is the book so many of us have been waiting for. In it, Harry Freedman explores, in an entrancingly original and totally accessible way, the spiritual inspiration that is such an integral part of Leonard's work. Beautifully written, this is among the finest volumes on Cohen's life and lyrics. It's an exploration which would have intrigued and engaged Leonard himself.'

John McKenna, writer and friend of Leonard Cohen

'An intriguing and specific look at the traditions and stories that influenced a brilliant songwriter.'

Library Journal

'There have been several books written about Cohen since his death but none of them, until now has gone deep into his soul. This is not a biography of the man but rather a biography of the landscape of his soul...Freedman explores song by song how Cohen reworked myths and prayers, legends and allegories and leads us to an understanding of Cohen's life as we gain insight into the man and his music.'

Reviews by Amos Lassen

'Freedman...takes a fresh approach by focusing on Biblical and Torahic references in Cohen's lyrics.'

Library Journal

'Harry Freedman's workmanlike examination of how Leonard Cohen's spiritual life shaped his songs is rich in detail.'

Tim Adams, *Observer New Review*

'...*The Mystical Roots of Genius* turned out to be a well-nigh perfect book to read over the High Holy Days... This is a charming and compelling walk through Leonard Cohen's spiritual life.'

Jenni Frazer, *Jewish Chronicle*

'Described on the flyleaf as "Britain's leading author of popular works of Jewish culture", Freedman lives up to his billing by expressing sharp scholarship in crisp sentences.'

'[Freedman's] handling of the words is masterly. He leaves you feeling wiser about Leonard Cohen, and Judaism, and life.'

Tim de Lisle, *The Tablet*

'Fluidly written...the breadth of Freedman's erudition is impressive. And ultimately he is an insightful guide to the many religious references in Cohen's back catalogue... Freedman has shone a light on the inspiration behind these songs. Much could have remained in darkness without him.'

Rory Kiberd, *Irish Independent*

'Freedman is a much-published Judaic and Aramaic scholar whose book brims with insight... The content of this book is terrific.'

David Kirby, *Independent* (app edition)

'This unique book is a gift to anyone who wishes to be accompanied more deeply into the biblical, Kabbalistic, and Buddhist themes underlying these texts.'

Church Times

'The redeeming power of Freedman's book is that it allows his fans to be exposed one more time to Cohen's incredible personality and intelligence and, for that reason, the book is a success.'

New York Journal of Books

'This book is for people who want to delve deeply into words of songs they may already know, admire and cherish.'

Jewish Libraries Reviews

'Freedman's knowledge of these sources is excellent ... stimulating.'

Spirituality & Practice

(Chosen for a Spirituality & Practice Book Award as one of the 50 Best Spiritual Books of 2021)

CONTENTS

LIST OF ILLUSTRATIONS

10 Cohen in concert at the O2 Arena, London,
     15 September 2013, part of his final world tour.
     (Brian Rasic/Getty Images)
11 Inauguration of Cohen's art exhibition at Oviedo
     University, October 2011. (Dusko Despotovic/
     Getty Images)
12 A mural of Leonard Cohen on a building in Crescent
     Street, Montreal, his home town. (Marc Braibant/
     AFP/Getty Images)

FOREWORD

Few contemporary songwriters have had their work dissected as minutely as Leonard Cohen. His lyrics have been picked apart innumerable times, in books and articles, on film and TV, in pubs, around dinner tables and on internet forums. PhD theses have been submitted exploring his philosophy, his impact on culture, his image as prophet and priest and much more. His work has been analysed from many different perspectives: psychologically, mystically, philosophically, spiritually, religiously and, not infrequently, incomprehensibly.

I have tried to do something different in this book. I have not attempted to guess what was going on in his mind when he wrote a particular song. He was said to be reluctant to encourage that. Nor have I dwelt in any greater depth on what motivated him. Rather, I have focused on his extensive use of biblical and religious traditions – ideas drawn from Judaism and Christianity that helped shape his identity and the way he made sense of the world. I have tried to demonstrate what his sources were, what their original context was, what the stories and ideas that lay behind them were and how Cohen harnessed them for his own purposes. The book is as much an exploration of his sources as of his work itself.

Leonard Cohen's work is so multifaceted that many of his songs are capable of more than one interpretation. Few of his pieces reflect a single theme, and hardly any originate from one idea alone. Most contain a wide range of images and allusions. Because this is a book about what lies behind his work, rather than an analysis of his compositions in their totality, I only look at those bits of his work which draw on the religious traditions the book explores. I skip lines or verses in the songs I am discussing if they do not contain this kind of material. The lines and verses that I discuss are printed in the text in bold type.

Cohen's knowledge of the Bible and religious folklore was profound: nearly everything he wrote contains something that touches on a religious idea, even if the song is in no way religious. It hasn't been practical to include all such glancing references. For example, *Tower of Song*, on the 1988 album *I'm Your Man*, is a humorous piece about a musician who is losing his mojo. There is nothing particularly religious about the song, other than the title, which refers to an obscure kabbalistic legend about seven towers in heaven, one of which was called the Tower of Song. King David was permitted to enter it, so long as he was singing.[1] We can assume that Cohen is referring to this legend, because he mentions twenty-seven angels who tie him to a table in the tower. But since there is nothing else to interest us mystically or religiously in the song, I haven't included it in the book.

For reasons of space I have not included any of the many poems that Cohen wrote. Not even *Book of Mercy*, his collection of psalms. I have concentrated on his music because that is what most people know him for. Maybe one day someone may decide to do something similar with his poetry.

Because it is possible to interpret so much of Leonard Cohen's work in more than one way, the opinions I state in this book can only be my personal view. You probably won't agree with everything I write. In fact I hope you don't; his work always holds out the likelihood of new insights. But hopefully some of what I have written will strike a chord, encouraging you to think about Leonard Cohen's music in a novel fashion.

After an introductory chapter on Leonard Cohen's influences I have divided the book into four parts, with a certain amount of overlap between them. The first, 'Bible as Allegory', explores songs where he has reshaped a biblical narrative to give it a new meaning, often with a contemporary relevance. 'Ideas from the Bible' is where he challenges the Bible, or our understanding of it, compares different approaches and attaches new meanings to biblical themes we often take for granted. In 'Heaven and Earth' I look at the mystical traditions that evolved out of the Bible, to the mechanics of Creation and the mysteries of the human soul. And finally, 'Prayer' is just that: conversations with whatever we conceive of as above, whether that be a conventional idea of God or something more ethereal.

For reasons of copyright I have not been able to print every song in full as I discuss them. However, Leonard Cohen's lyrics are freely available in many different places on the internet, for example at Jarkko Arjatsalo's superb website leonardcohenfiles.com. You may wish to refer to it as you read this book.

I have tried as much as possible to avoid using technical language when describing the sources that lie behind Cohen's religious work. But there are a few terms that need to be explained. We will refer occasionally to the Talmud, or Talmudic stories. The Talmud is the ancient, 2-million-word, multi-volume repository of Jewish law, belief, customs, history, legend and folklore. It is the primary text of *rabbinic* Judaism, the Judaism found in synagogues today. Some rabbinic legends and folklore are contained in literary collections other than the Talmud; these collections are known as *midrash*. Finally, Kabbalah is the Jewish mystical tradition that goes back to biblical times but which reached the peak of its development between the thirteenth and the sixteenth centuries. Its most important text, compiled in twelfth-century Spain, is the Zohar. Kabbalah also found its way into Christianity and gained a new popularity in the secular New Age of the late twentieth century.

INTRODUCTION

Leonard Cohen never planned to be a rock star. He had ambitions to be a novelist or, better still, to be recognized for his greatest love, his poetry. In his youth the idea of setting his words to music rarely crossed his mind. And even when it did, and he started writing songs for others, the thought of performing them himself positively terrified him. So much so that the first time he was asked to perform his music in public he got stage fright and darted off midway through his act.

Cohen was born at the autumn equinox, on 21 September 1934, into an affluent and well-regarded middle-class family in Montreal. The Cohens were one of the oldest Jewish families in Canada. It was probably assumed that Leonard would continue in the family traditions of commerce and communal activity. It is what the family had done ever since his great-grandfather Lazarus left Poland in 1869, settling in the small town of Maberly in Ontario. Lazarus had been a rabbi in the old country, where he would have been known as Eliezer, or Lazar (pronounced 'laser') for short. At his circumcision Cohen was given the Hebrew name Eliezer in his great-grandfather's memory.

When he arrived in Canada, Lazarus gave up his career with the old prophets and turned to new profits. He transformed himself from rabbi to businessman, moving in the 1880s to Montreal, where he established a brass foundry and twice became president of the city's synagogue. His brother Tzvi Hirsch stuck with the prophets, becoming the unofficial Chief Rabbi of Canada.

Lazarus's son Lyon, Leonard Cohen's paternal grandfather, inherited his father's commercial talents. He owned a successful clothing business and founded the first Jewish newspaper in Canada, the *Jewish Times*. An aim of the paper was to encourage Canada's burgeoning Jewish immigrant population to integrate quickly and successfully into the local community, to abandon their old Eastern European superstitions in favour of a more refined Canadian outlook.

As scholarly and communally active as his father, whom he succeeded as president of the synagogue, Lyon held many senior leadership roles in the Canadian Jewish community. He set up a fund to assist Jewish victims of the Russian pogroms, established a committee to resettle their refugees in Canada, built a community centre and served as governor of several hospitals and schools. He eventually became the President of the Canadian Jewish Congress, effectively making him the lay leader of the country's Jewish community.

Scholarly and with an aristocratic bearing, Lyon Cohen travelled to Rome in 1924 to meet Pope Pius XI on behalf of Canada's Jews, but was taken ill before the meeting could take place. He hosted leading statesmen and religious leaders in his home, among them Chaim Weizmann, the first president of the future state of Israel. The Cohens were considered to be aristocracy in the eyes of Montreal's immigrant Jewish community. The expectations riding on Leonard Cohen, who was only two when his grandfather died, must have been immense.

When the First World War broke out, the staunchly patriotic Lyon Cohen set up a recruitment drive to encourage young Jewish men to enlist in the Canadian Armed Forces. Among the first to enrol were his sons Horace and Nathan, Leonard Cohen's father. Nathan returned from the war in poor health. He carried on the family clothing business, but his infirmity meant that he generally played second fiddle in the company to his brother Horace. Nathan died in 1943, when Leonard Cohen was only nine years old.

Cohen's mother, Masha, came from a family as committed to their Jewish roots as were the Cohens. Her father, Rabbi Solomon Klonitzky-Kline, had been born in Lithuania, where during the First World War he had been the principal of a *yeshiva,* a Talmudic college, in the large Jewish community of Kovno. Life was not easy for the impoverished Lithuanian Jews, and when a wave of pogroms broke out in the 1920s, making their existence even more perilous, he left to join one of his daughters living in the United States. His other daughter, Masha, Cohen's mother, was already in Canada, working as a nurse. When her work permit ran out, her father got in touch with the committee that Lyon Cohen had set up to help settle Jewish refugees. That was how she and Nathan met.

After Nathan and Masha married, Rabbi Klonitzky-Kline settled down to write his magnum opus. Written in Hebrew with a title that translates as *A Treasury of Rabbinic Interpretations*, it was a compilation of thousands of ancient insights into the Torah. Culled from the vast library of rabbinic literature written between the second and the seventh centuries, the book was published in New York in 1939.[1] It was his second book: the first, a dictionary of Hebrew homonyms, had been published a few years earlier. He was in the process of writing another dictionary when he died. Cohen recalled that he was doing so without consulting any other reference work; he just started at the first letter, *aleph*, and worked his way through.

Cohen inherited his love of learning and his easy familiarity with Jewish tradition from both sides of the family. He also inherited a sense that it was important to dress well. Frequently pictured in a suit and tie, and never looking like a *shlok*,[2] Leonard Cohen was always the best-dressed performer on the rock circuit. And probably the most polite as well.

Leonard Cohen was in his teens when his grandfather, by now an old man, came to live with them in Montreal. He recalled how he would study with him, working through the book of Isaiah together. He described how his elderly grandfather would nod off mid-sentence until, waking up with a start, his finger would fly back to the beginning of the passage they had concluded a few minutes earlier. But, despite living in the same house and studying together, Cohen once said that he didn't feel that he knew his grandfather very well. He said that he didn't consider him to be a continuing influence on his life.

Elegant, musical, warm-hearted, dramatic and volatile, Masha Cohen found the death of her husband difficult to cope with. Left to bring up Cohen and his older sister, Esther, on her own, she suffered from bouts of melancholy, which transmuted into depression as she grew older, a trait that Leonard Cohen shared. He endured periods of depression for much of his life; they didn't leave him until he was well into his sixties.

4

Cohen's childhood was materially secure and stable. Part of a tightly knit extended family, Cohen, his mother and sister lived in a big house with domestic help and structured routines. He went to Hebrew school on Sunday mornings and two afternoons each week. It was quite an intense religious regime but not unusual in those days for families whose Jewish identity was as important to them as their Canadian one.

Long after the deaths of Lazarus and Lyon Cohen, the family were still at the heart of the Montreal Jewish community. When the young Cohen went to synagogue with his uncles, they would sit together in the same prominent seats that the clan had always occupied. But as he grew older and began to make a name for himself as a poet, his relationship with the community started to waver. It hit rock bottom when he gave a speech at Montreal's Jewish Public Library in 1963. He condemned the community's religious practices as fossilized, mechanical and lacking in spirituality. 'I believe we have eliminated all but the most blasphemous ideas of God,' he said. 'I believe that the God worshipped in our synagogues is a hideous distortion of a supreme idea – and deserves to be attacked and destroyed. I consider it one of my duties to expose the platitude which we have created.'[3]

His disdain for what he saw as the soulless rigidity of the established Jewish community led Cohen to speculate on the emergence of a new, underground spiritual entity, something he referred to as a 'catacomb religion'. In a 1967 interview he said:

Everybody has a sense that they are in their own capsule and the one that I have always been in, for want of a better word, is that of cantor – a priest of a catacomb religion that is underground, just beginning, and I am one of the many singers, one of the many priests, not by any means a high priest, but one of the creators of the liturgy that will create the church.[4]

It was quite an ambition, one that didn't come to fruition in the way he imagined.

Leonard Cohen was reluctant in interviews to discuss the religious aspects of his work or performances. He didn't like the suggestion that his music might have a spiritual purpose. He rarely went into any sort of detail about his own religious practices, though he did often say that he lit Sabbath candles on a Friday evening. But his name, Cohen, indicated that he was a member of the priestly caste, a descendant of the biblical Aaron. When he was first told this as a child, 'I believed. I wanted to wear white clothes, and to go into the Holy of Holies, and negotiate with the deepest resources of my soul.' There are not many children who are conscious of their souls, let alone suspect that they contain deep resources.[5]

For over 40 years, beginning in the early 1970s, Leonard Cohen spent much of his time at the Buddhist monastery at Mount Baldy in California. His commitment to the monastery and to his teacher, Joshu Sasaki Roshi, was a defining aspect of his life. Once, on a night run when staying at the monastery, he tripped over a low stone wall and damaged his knees. As a result, he couldn't perform the exercises necessary for his meditations. Instead, he picked up the bag of *tefillin* (small

leather boxes containing Torah verses, worn during prayer)
that he had inherited from his grandfather.

> And I wondered 'What is this thing, what are these
> morning prayers?' And I began to look into them, and to
> study them, and to say them, and to try to penetrate them.
> And to try to make sense of them, in the deepest way ... I
> saw how exquisite and skilful these prayers were, how they
> had been designed by minds that you have to incline your
> head toward. These minds who designed these prayers or
> received the inspiration to design these prayers – these are
> incredibly subtle and exquisite prayers for lifting the soul.[6]

He began wearing his *tefillin* in the early morning, and saying
the daily prayers. Shortly after this, he produced *Book of
Mercy*, his most overtly Jewish work, a book of 50 psalms. He
described it as a secret book for him; a book of prayer, a sacred
kind of conversation.[7]

Jews tend to be fairly reserved about expressing their
religious commitment, and Cohen was no exception. He
was reluctant to talk about what it meant to him to be a Jew,
explaining it only through the lens of Kabbalah, rather than on
a personal level:

> I don't like to be identified with Jewish thought. In my own
> mind I know that I am deeply conditioned by it. One of the
> great themes of kabbalistic thought is the idea that the thrust
> of Jewish activity is the repair of God. God, in creating the

world, dispersed itself; creation is a catastrophe, there are pieces of him, or her, or it, that are everywhere, in fact, and the specific task of the Jew is to repair the face of God.[8]

Although he was reluctant to describe his work as having a religious or spiritual purpose, there is no doubt about the spiritual quest in Cohen's music and poetry. The spirit is by no means his only theme: love, sex, humour and even war also feature prominently. But his religious outlook is notable because it reflects his outlook on life, the way he understood the contemporary human condition. His religion was not bound up in formal ritual observance, nor did he make a point of advocating the performance of religious virtues such as justice and charity; these are in any case written into the social contract nowadays. Cohen's religion was introspective and experiential, a way of engaging with the yearnings of his soul, a space for self-examination and spiritual quest. Suffering periods of depression and dark moods, he used his poetry and lyrics to make sense of what he saw as a broken world. Speaking in 1990 of his song *The War*, he said: 'Even in the midst of this flood, or catastrophe, which we are in, these are the days of the flood, these are the final days, in a sense all the institutions are, and have been swept away and the ethical question is, what is the proper behaviour, what is the appropriate behaviour in the midst of a catastrophe?'[9]

I

LEONARD COHEN'S INFLUENCES

We'd be hard pressed to listen to any Leonard Cohen song, or read any of his poems, and not find something in it that seems to have a religious connotation. Not that the religious significance is always immediately obvious: it can easily pass us by if we are not paying enough attention. Sometimes the religious content is so obscure that it can't even be detected in the lyrics; it exists only in the idea that led to the song in the first place, or in the subliminal message that the song is trying to get across.

Cohen said that when he began writing *I Can't Forget*, which he recorded on the *I'm Your Man* album, he imagined it would be

> a song about the exodus of the Hebrew children from Egypt, which was intended as a metaphor for the freeing of the soul from bondage. When I went in to record the vocal for the track, however, I found I couldn't get the words out of my throat. I couldn't sing the words because I wasn't entitled to speak of the emancipation of the spirit.[1]

As he struggled to write the song he found that, instead of developing the original theme, he was asking questions of himself, struggling with what he thought he knew and what he was really capable of telling anyone. As he thought it through, he came to the realization that he had to go back to basics and challenge himself. He needed to discover his purpose, work out what he was trying to achieve with his life. By the time the song finally emerged it had changed completely from its original idea of freeing the soul from bondage. It had become a song about a man stumbling out of bed, getting ready for the struggle of the day, not believing in himself, knowing there was something he must not forget but unable to remember what it was. If what counts is the idea behind a song, then *I Can't Forget*, which began as a composition based on a biblical story, remains religious. Even though there is not a word of conventional religion in it.[2]

Cohen's grandfather may have been too old to be an active influence on him when they studied Isaiah together, but the Bible was always part of his life. When his son Adam was critically ill, in a coma following a car crash, Cohen sat by his bed for four months. Sometimes he read passages to him from the Bible. When Adam came round, the first thing he said was, 'Dad can you read something else?'[3]

Cohen would say that his familiarity with the Bible originated from his childhood in Montreal, where he was surrounded by religious symbols. But it is not the biblical symbols and stories he draws on that challenge us when we hear his lyrics. What strikes us when we listen to him is the way that he uses biblical imagery to deliver messages often far removed from their original biblical setting. *Story of Isaac* is transformed by Cohen from its biblical context, a test of Abraham's religious fanaticism, into a protest about the way people are willing to sacrifice others for absurd ideals. *Born in Chains*, a song that sounds as if it is about the Exodus from Egypt, becomes a sanctification of human love. And *Hallelujah*, his most famous song, drawing on several biblical narratives, becomes a meditation on the paradoxical nature of words, both their holiness and their impiety.

Cohen's religious imagery is not confined to the Bible; indeed direct biblical allusions account for only a small proportion of his work. Deeply spiritual, he delved into a wide variety of mystical and occult disciplines. But more often than not, when he used religious imagery in his compositions, he drew on Christian and Jewish sources: the messianic hope of the New Testament, the mysticism of the Kabbalah and the folklore of the Talmud and Midrash. He was not a Talmudist in the conventional sense of the word – he did not devote his life to decoding the complex logic of Talmudic arguments – but he carried the cultured and educated Jewish environment of his childhood with him. He knew the Bible, read the religious philosophy of Martin Buber and the academic mysticism of Gershom Scholem, conversed with rabbis, studied Adin Steinsaltz's ground-breaking editions of the Talmud and was familiar with Daniel Matt's translation of the Zohar. He knew many Talmudic stories and could quote its aphorisms, even if his eyes had not necessarily alighted on the particular page they originally came from.

Sometimes, but less often than we might imagine, Cohen harnesses these sources to create new narratives, creating modern folk tales by using ancient motifs. More commonly he composes prayers, hymns and psalms, or develops the mystical hints of Kabbalah to offer perspectives on the soul, or on the nature of God.

The Holocaust had a powerful impact on his work. He was 11 years old when pictures of the newly liberated concentration camps started to appear, with their images of emaciated, swollen-bellied, dull-eyed victims. His song *Dance Me to the End of Love* has a line about burning violins. He told the audience at a concert in Cologne in 1988 that the song arose from a photograph he had seen, of people in striped concentration camp uniforms being forced to play violins as victims were herded into gas chambers.

Leonard Cohen was never constrained by the sources he drew on. Even when he is influenced by a biblical narrative or legend, the piece he writes is unlikely to be rooted in that legend alone. There are always multiple influences at play in what he writes, and nearly every one of his compositions is open to alternative interpretations. So there is nothing monochrome about his work. To explore the religious ideas and folklore that lie behind so much of his work, to form our own insights into the man and his thought, it is useful to know a little more about the people, ideas and texts that helped shape him.

The spiritual discipline that had the greatest effect on Cohen's life, perhaps even more than his childhood exposure to Judaism and Christianity, was the Rinzai form of Zen Buddhism which he learned from the Japanese Zen master Joshu Sasaki Roshi, the guiding light of his life. Cohen spent a considerable amount of time, over several decades, at Roshi's monastery on California's Mount Baldy. Eventually he moved into the monastery permanently and in 1996, after he had been there for three years, he was ordained as a Buddhist monk.

It seems from the interviews he gave that Cohen's main motivation in studying Zen, and eventually becoming a monk, was not so much the discipline of Zen itself as his relationship with Roshi: 'I liked what he said, and I liked who he was and I began to study with him ... And I suppose if he had been a professor of physics in Heidelberg I would have learned German and studied physics, but he happened to be an old monk, so I began to study with him in his own terms.'[4]

It is not surprising that there are very few uniquely Zen allusions in Leonard Cohen's work; Zen is a contemplative discipline aiming at enlightenment, a way of being rather than a system of belief and lifestyle. It didn't provide him with a theology, a historiography or a mythology in the same way as Christianity and Judaism did. He never saw a conflict between Buddhism and Judaism, explaining that in Zen 'there is no prayerful worship and there is no discussion of a deity'.[5]

A direct and potent influence on Cohen's lyrics and verse was the Spanish poet and playwright Federico García Lorca (1898–1936). Lorca was a significant figure in the Spanish avant-garde of the early twentieth century. Born into a well-off family, he received a good education but found himself unable to commit to academic study; his early ambition was to become a musician and composer. At the age of 19 he moved to Madrid's Residencia de Estudiantes, a vibrant and progressive residential cultural centre, where he became friendly with Salvador Dalí and the film-maker Luis Buñuel. Lorca's poetry expresses in words the same surrealistic perception of the world that Dalí and Buñuel convey visually. He opposed the growing fascist movement in Spain, making no secret of his left-wing views, or of the fact that he was gay. In 1936 he was arrested by Franco's soldiers and executed a few days later. He was 38 years old.

Cohen first came across Lorca's work in 1950, while he was still a teenager. He was browsing in a second-hand bookshop when he picked up Lorca's *Selected Poems*. Cohen was astonished both by Lorca's sensuous style and by his direct, graphic imagery. The book had fallen open at an evocative love poem, 'Gacela of the Morning Market'. On stage, Cohen would often recite its opening lines:

Through the Arch of Elvira,
I want to see you go,
So that I can learn your name,
And break into tears.

'Lorca,' said Cohen, 'led me into the racket of poetry. He educated me. He taught me to understand the dignity of sorrow through flamenco music, and to be deeply touched by the dance image of a Gypsy man and woman. Thanks to him, Spain entered my mind at 15, and later I became inflamed by the civil war leftist folk song music.'[6] Echoes of Lorca's work can be heard throughout Cohen's portfolio. His song *Take*

This Waltz is his translation of Lorca's poem *Pequeño vals vienés*. Leonard Cohen and his wife, Suzanne Elrod, named their daughter Lorca.

Cohen also spoke of his fascination with the medieval Persian poet Jalal-ud-din Rumi. Although their worlds could not have been more different, Cohen understood Rumi's intense spirituality and sense of displacement, of being a stranger in a host culture not wholly one's own. Rumi, who was born in 1207, grew up in a scholarly family in Tajikstan. Forced to flee their home as a result of a Mongol invasion, his family wandered for many years before finally settling in Konya, in Anatolia, now part of Turkey. At the age of 24 he succeeded his father as a teacher of theology in one of the town's madrassahs. In November 1244 he met a wandering dervish, Shams-al-din, in the streets of Konya. Under his direction he began to study the mysteries of the higher worlds.

The two men began to live together, drawing so spiritually close to each other that Rumi began to neglect his family, his responsibilities and his work. Scandalized, Rumi's family conspired to drive the dervish out of town, forcing him back to his native Syria. Rumi was heartbroken, and his eldest son could not bear to see his father in such a state. He brought Shams back from Syria, incensing the rest of the family even more. In 1247 Shams disappeared for ever. He'd been murdered, probably by Rumi's other sons.

Grief-stricken, Rumi found his solace in poetry. He expressed his spiritual love for Shams in verse, attaching the dervish's name to much of his work. His poetry expresses the beauty of nature, cloaked in religious and mystical imagery. He was, according to Leonard Cohen, 'in the same league as King David'.[7]

In the liner notes for the 1979 album *Recent Songs*, Cohen wrote that he owed his thanks to his childhood friend 'Robert Hershorn, who, many years ago, put into my hands the books of the old Persian poets Attar and Rumi, whose imagery influenced several songs, especially *The Guests* and *The Window*'. Ten years later he told the story of an American woman who had studied Sufi dance in Iran and was now teaching it in the United States. A Persian friend, visiting Sufi groups in America, told her that in his country Sufis were dancing to a song, written by a Westerner, which 'had the spirit of Rumi in it'. The song, he said, was Leonard Cohen's *The Guests*.

Not all of Cohen's influences had a direct impact on his literary style. Some of his most important role models were those who encouraged him in his work, setting him off on his path as a poet or impelling him to think more closely about what he was trying to achieve with his poetry. The most powerful of these was Cohen's lifelong friend, the poet Irving Layton. A Montreal Jew like Cohen, though 20 years older, in his heyday Layton had been regarded as Canada's outstanding poet.

Layton received a host of international garlands, including the Canadian Governor General's Award and Italy's Petrarch Prize. He was twice nominated for the Nobel Prize for literature. He encouraged Cohen when he was beginning to write, admitting him into the small select band of young Montreal poets of which Layton was the leading light, and publishing him for the first time in the magazine that the group produced, devoted to Canadian poetry. He and Cohen became close friends, Layton's outgoing, flamboyant personality acting as a foil to the younger man's quiet introspection.

Layton was a far more experienced poet than Cohen. He had taught in several universities and published a significant body of work, but he was never Cohen's teacher. He encouraged Cohen in his poetry, but he didn't teach him how to be a poet. Cohen, who regarded Layton as the finest writer that Canada had ever produced, said that he didn't feel he had been influenced by him in a literary sense. Rather, Layton had enlightened the process of writing poetry for him.

He said something similar about another Montreal poet, Louis Dudek. Like Layton, Dudek strove to establish a native tradition of poetry in Canada, a style that was unique to their country. 'Give us five hundred readers,' he would say, 'and we will give you a literature.' Dudek taught Leonard Cohen at McGill University, and in 1956 his McGill Poetry Series published Cohen's first poetry collection, *Let Us Compare Mythologies*. Cohen described Dudek as a magnificent teacher, although he wasn't overawed, either by the man or by his reputation. 'Back then I was very self-confident. I had no doubts that my work would penetrate the world painlessly. I believed that I was among the great.'[8]

It was under Dudek's tutelage that Cohen began to seriously think of himself as a poet. Once, after reading one of Cohen's poems, Dudek spontaneously 'knighted' him as a poet, using a rolled-up newspaper. But eventually Dudek became disillusioned with Cohen's poetry. He criticized him for his 'obscure cosmological imagery ... a rag bag of classical mythology'. Cohen, wrote Dudek, belonged to a young generation of poets who were 'not even capable of social anger or pity'. When he read this, Layton leapt to Cohen's defence. He called Dudek's attitude 'as stupid as it is false. Cohen is one of the purest lyrical talents this country has ever produced.'[9]

A third Montreal poet, A. M. Klein, unwittingly had a career-changing impact on Cohen's self-perception as a poet. Klein was a leading figure in the Canadian-Jewish literary world; Leonard Cohen had grown up reading his work. He'd even written two poems about Klein before the two men ever met. But Klein had struggled to make a living as a poet and had been obliged to take jobs that were peripheral to his art, doing little to advance his literary reputation. He had edited the *Canadian Jewish Chronicle* and worked as a speech writer to the businessman and philanthropist Samuel Bronfman. By the time Leonard Cohen first met him, A. M. Klein was on the verge of the nervous breakdown that would cut short his writing career. It was a breakdown that made Cohen realize the extent of the sacrifice that Klein had made for his art.

In his speech in 1963 at the Montreal Jewish Public Library, where he antagonized the communal leadership and their stalwarts, Cohen blamed Klein's breakdown on the destructive influence of the Jewish community. Their indifference to artists, he said, had effectively exiled Klein. Obsessed with business and institutions, the community had shunned those who loved the old traditions of scholarship and learning.

Klein, he said, had tried to act as a priest to the community, to preserve the old ways, but he had been alone in his nostalgia for the past. This led to Klein's loneliness, his isolation, his breakdown. 'He spoke to men who despised the activity he loved most. He chose to be a priest and protect the dead ritual. And now we have his silence.' What the community needed, thundered Cohen, was a prophet, not a priest: a prophet who follows ideas, as they fluctuate, change, mutate, 'trying never to mistake the cast-off shell with the swift-changing thing that shed it'. Cohen learned from the decline of A. M. Klein that this role of prophet now fell to him. He would have to go into exile, he resolved, 'thinking up other possibilities for spiritual life; possibilities like love and sex and drugs and song, for which there was little room in the synagogue'.[10]

Love and sex and drugs and song. They are all there in Cohen's music. He once claimed to know nothing about love, to have no thoughts about it.

> I don't think too much. I never think, to tell you the truth. My own personal life is chaotic. Anybody who looks at my own personal life will come to the conclusion that I don't think at all … I generally respond to it in real life in exactly the wrong way of doing things. As a friend of mine once said: 'Now, Leonard, are you sure you are doing the wrong thing?'[11]

But of course, he did know about love. We can't listen to his masterpieces like *Suzanne*, *A Thousand Kisses Deep* or *So Long,*

Marianne and think: this is someone who knows nothing about love.

He may have thought he knew nothing about love, but he admitted that he had been completely obsessed with women even since he could remember. A friend said that both he and Cohen had 'a thirst for and attraction to, the opposite sex in all of its varieties, and with it the dream of some ideal woman … All of Leonard's erotic poetry bears the seal of this longing.'[12] Erotic, graphic, romantic: Cohen's love songs are almost unique in the respectful way they combine all three. And yet these are not the songs of a chart-topping rock star singing about love for a teenage audience that rarely thinks about anything else. There is no contradiction between the explicit eroticism of some of his lyrics and his saintly spirituality. Love for Cohen was sacred, the physical counterpart of the human quest for the divine. 'I decided to worship beauty the way some people go back to the religion of their fathers.'[13] There is no conflict between religion and love in Leonard Cohen's music, any more than there is in the sublime, erotic Song of Songs, understood by church and synagogue as a metaphor for divine love. Sex can be a religious act.

Not completely though. There is little religious about the bawdy, humorous *Don't Go Home with Your Hard-On*. The song appears on *Death of a Ladies' Man*, the album that Cohen recorded in Phil Spector's chaotic, drunken studio. As if the title was not outrageous enough, just as they began the recording Bob Dylan burst in, accompanied by two women and a bottle of whisky. Then Allen Ginsberg and his lover arrived. They all joined in, a spontaneous, discordant, boozy backing group, Spector manically directing them, crying out that there were enough Jews in the room for a bar mitzvah. The heavy, pulsating, over-produced track that resulted, with its enthusiastic, raucous vocals, is perhaps the least typical of all Leonard Cohen's songs. If asked to nominate a Leonard Cohen track that most deserved to be recorded by the cream of Jewish America's musical and literary talent in 1970, *Don't Go Home with Your Hard-On* is the one we'd be least likely to think of.

So sex didn't have to be religious. But it can be. Coition is the first thing to be mandated by the Bible: Adam and Eve were commanded to be fruitful and multiply, to become one flesh. As Cohen told an interviewer: 'In the Jewish tradition ... both the procreational and recreational aspects of sexual activity are affirmed.'[14] The Kabbalah stresses the mystical essentiality of sex; the conjunction of male and female anticipates the mystical union of the human and the divine. Of all Cohen's sexual imagery the line that best illustrates his belief in sex as a divine activity occurs, appropriately, in *Hallelujah*: 'I remember when I moved in you, and the Holy Dove she was moving too.'

Drugs were important too. Not so much in his lyrics – references to drugs are few and far between and tend to be humorous when they do occur – but Cohen used a lot of recreational drugs, particularly when he was younger. He found that LSD and marijuana helped his creativity, gave him the courage to go on stage in the early days and helped him deal with depression. They could also serve as a substitute for religion, 'to liberate spiritual energy... Thanks to drugs I could consider myself as the Great Evangelist of the New Age.'[15]

For a while he used amphetamines to help with his writing; he told his biographer that his mental and physical processes were so slow that speed brought him up to a normal tempo. Then he would take Mandrax to help him come down from the speed. He never became seriously addicted, a reprieve for which he gave thanks to his weak stomach. It would never allow him to retain the quantities necessary for addiction.

Cohen's early recordings attracted a certain amount of derision from those more used to the upbeat, punchy tunes of the 1960s. They called it dreary, dirge-like, music to kill yourself by. But humour runs through his work, particularly as he got older. 'I remember what Ben Jonson said: "I've studied all the philosophies and theologies but cheerfulness keeps breaking through."' One of the qualities that make Cohen's music accessible is that, no matter how dark the subject, he is able to leaven it with humour – even in his early work, when he was most at his dirge-like.

Even if his humour did not break through so much in his early work, it was never far beneath the surface. In a review of his 1972 poetry collection *The Energy of Slaves* Jeremy Robson recalled hearing of a TV interview that Cohen had given when much younger to a condescending interviewer:

'Tell me, Mr. Cohen,' she'd asked, 'have you ever
    considered changing your name?'
'Why, yes,' came the reflective reply. 'Often.'

'To what?'

'To September.'

The woman smiled triumphantly. 'Leonard September,' she mouthed.

'No!' the young poet shot back. 'September Cohen.'[16]

Certain themes and topics recur in Cohen's songs. One, which may surprise us, is the attention he pays to war. Not because he wants to glorify it, but because of the extreme demands that war makes. 'War is wonderful,' he once told an interviewer.

> They'll never stamp it out. It's one of the few times people can act their best. It's so economical in terms of gesture and motion, every single gesture is precise, every effort is at its maximum. Nobody goofs off. Everybody is responsible for his brother. The sense of community and kinship and brotherhood, devotion. There are opportunities to feel things that you simply cannot feel in modern city life.[17]

The appeal that war held for Cohen is partly explained by his father Nathan's experiences in the First World War, conditioned by the insistence of his own father that young Jewish Canadians should make a point of putting themselves forward in the armed forces. Nathan had kept his service revolver from the war, engraved with his name rank and regiment. As a child, Cohen was fascinated by it.

Leonard Cohen was five years old when the Second World War broke out. One of his childhood friends recalls how big an event the war was in their young minds. Everyone knew somebody who had gone to war, had heard of someone who had been wounded or killed. Montreal's Jews were gripped by the terrible fear that Canada might lose and that the Nazis might take over. And at the same time there was an expectation that 'when the war ended, after all the sacrifices, the world was going to become this wonderful utopian place, with all this collective energy that had been dissipated in the war directed towards its creation'.[18]

He flew to Cuba in 1961, in the build-up to the Bay of Pigs crisis, when the world was poised on the brink of nuclear war. While he was there, he dressed in khaki fatigues and grew a beard in tribute to Che Guevara. When the Americans invaded, he was arrested on the beach by a dozen soldiers, who assumed the bearded foreigner was one of the invaders. Cohen turned on the charm, stammered out a few sentences in broken Spanish and told them that he was a friend of the people. The soldiers, realizing he was harmless, poured him a glass of rum, gave him a necklace made of shells, hugged him and let him go.

Cohen's preoccupation with war led him into a dangerous confrontation on stage in Hamburg. It was 4 May 1970, and news had just come through that in the USA the National Guard had opened fire on anti-war protesters at Kent State University, killing four unarmed students and wounding nine. Cohen was in a dark place. He was playing a gig in Germany, bombed out on the hypnotic sedative Mandrax. He began the second half of his act by goose-stepping, lifting his arm and crying 'Sieg Heil'. The crowd erupted in rage, shouting and throwing things, one of them reportedly charging the stage with a gun. Cohen picked up his guitar and the crowd went quiet. He provoked them again by breaking into an old Yiddish song. The crowd erupted once more. Things didn't calm down until he played one of his own pieces that the audience could join in with. After the gig his backing group threatened to quit. They didn't; instead they became known as The Army.

In 1973, when the Yom Kippur War broke out between Israel and its Arab neighbours, Cohen flew to Tel Aviv, where he joined a small medley of performers who entertained the troops. Although he was partly motivated by a feeling that he should do something to help Israel, he was equally reacting to the turmoil of his relationship at the time with Suzanne Elrod, the mother of his children. 'Because it is so horrible between us I will go and stop Egypt's bullet,' he wrote.[19] Those who were with him recall him wanting to be drafted, to serve as a paratrooper, marine or pilot.

He was taken to Suez, and performed with his troupe for small groups of soldiers around the canal and the Red Sea. He later told an interviewer about the impact his visit had on him: 'I've never disguised the fact that I'm Jewish and in any crisis in Israel I would be there. I was there in the last war and I would be there in another war. … You get caught up in the thing. And the desert is beautiful and you think your life is meaningful for a moment or two.'[20]

But the real war that Cohen wanted to fight was not between opposing military forces. After his visit to Cuba he wrote to his brother-in-law explaining that the outcome of the war he was fighting

> is more important than the temporary and perhaps fictitious struggle between East and West. It is the war between those who conceive of existence as a dynamic rainbow, and those who conceive of it as a grey monotone, between those who are willing to acknowledge the endless possibilities, agonies, delights, mysteries and destinies of the human predicament, and those who meet every human question with a rigid set of answers ... This is the old war, Athens against Sparta, Socrates against Athens, Isaiah against the priests, the war that deeply involves 'our western civilization', the one to which I am committed.[21]

Cohen's war was a spiritual and cultural confrontation, a battle for the human soul.

Cohen's attraction to the idea of war, whether physical or philosophical, partly explains his interest in Joan of Arc. Her name crops up in three of his poems, and the final track on his *Songs of Love and Hate* album is devoted to her. He once said that he was fascinated by Joan of Arc because 'from the point of view of the woman's movement she really does stand for something stunningly original and courageous'. But of course there have been many courageous women in history; what makes Joan of Arc almost unique among them is that she drew her courage from her religious conviction, displayed it on the battlefield and ended up as a martyr.[22]

Joan of Arc lived in France during the final phase of the Hundred Years War, when the country was under English domination. As a teenager she experienced visions instructing her to drive the English from the land. She was told to take the Dauphin, the heir to the French throne, to Reims, where he would be crowned.

Although the French nobles were initially reluctant to take her seriously, her appearance on the battlefield led to a change in the nation's fortunes. She led the army to several victories, until she was eventually captured by the English and put on trial. She was burned at the stake in 1431. Five hundred years later she was canonized by the Roman Catholic Church.

In telling her story, Cohen visualizes her as pursued by flames as she rides alone through the dark, moonless night. She has no man to keep her warm. The picture he paints is of bright, murderous fire pursuing the armed yet vulnerable woman. She says she is tired of the war, she wishes to return to her former life. She yearns for a wedding dress, to be a woman once more, for something to cover her 'swollen appetite'.

When the fire hears her plea, he declares his love for her solitude and pride. Joan is instantly seduced, telling the fire to make his body cold as she climbs inside, making herself his bride. As the fire takes her ashes into his heart Joan cries, but her eyes shine with glory. Finally we hear Leonard Cohen's voice. He too longs for love and for light, but must it be so cruel?

Cohen's treatment of Joan of Arc's life is a gallery of his favourite themes. We have a woman, war, fire, despair, love,

LEONARD COHEN

sexual metaphor, the embrace of the carnal by the immaterial. We are bombarded by polarities in collision: fire and wood, war and love, dark and flame, cold fire, glory shining from an ashen eye.

The only thing missing from his catalogue of familiar tropes seems to be an overtly religious or biblical image. But if religion includes a belief in destiny, then religion is there, in the opening lines, with the flames pursuing Joan of Arc, her ultimate fate already determined, pursuing her, just waiting for its moment. As Cohen explained it: 'I was thinking … of this sense of a destiny that human beings have and how they meet and marry their destiny, how ultimately there is, you know, a male or a minus-plus, however you want to put it, you know a positive-negative yin-yang, male-female.'[23]

Cohen is in no doubt that the whole song is nothing if not religious: 'It was a strange song indeed,' he said, 'it was out of myself and contained the notion of reverence. When I recorded that song I will admit to having a strong religious feeling. I don't think it'll happen again.'[24]

In 2004 Cohen received a phone call from his daughter Lorca at his Montreal apartment. A friend had told her that Cohen should take a look at his bank account. To his horror, he discovered that it had been almost completely cleaned out. His manager, a trusted friend and former lover, had, it was alleged, been embezzling money from him. More than $5 million had disappeared from his account.

He hadn't been aware of what had been going on. He'd trusted his manager, Kelley Lynch, with his money and paid little attention to his affairs, and for a good part of the previous decade he had been relatively cut off from the world, living in the Buddhist monastery on Mount Baldy, California. He sued Lynch and won the case, but the money was not repaid. Instead Lynch began a campaign of harassment against him which only ended when she was sentenced to a term in prison. But Leonard Cohen was broke, and although his lawyers managed to recoup some of his money, at the age of 77 he was obliged to resume his musical career. Despite collapsing on stage at a concert in Spain, he played 387 concerts over five years to sell-out audiences throughout the world, and made three new albums.

He died in 2016, his timing immaculate. The following day Donald Trump won the US presidential election. The broken world he sang about had fractured even further.

THE BIBLE AS ALLEGORY

Whither thou goest, I will go,
Wherever thou lodgest I will lodge,
Thy people shall be my people ...[1]

Leonard Cohen and his backing singers chanted these lines as they bade farewell to the audience at his July 2008 concert in London's O2 arena. Taken from the biblical book of Ruth, they are the vow that the widowed Ruth made to her mother-in-law when she refused to abandon Naomi and return to her parents' home. Cohen didn't offer an introduction to these lines, and he said nothing about them. Perhaps significantly, he omitted the final clause in Ruth's vow, 'Thy God will be my God.'

Although biblical ideas and language run all the way through Cohen's work, he rarely quoted directly from the Bible in the way he did with Ruth's vow. Nor did he often retell biblical stories. But we frequently hear echoes of Bible stories woven into other lyrics. There's the itinerant hoping to strike lucky in *The Stranger Song*, who was 'just some Joseph looking for a manger', and the seeker who is advised in *Steer Your Way* to find a route 'through the fables of Creation and the Fall'. Despite its title, *Sisters of Mercy* is not a tale about nuns: it's a song about two young women who offered Cohen a place to stay for the night when he had nowhere else to go.

Sometimes Cohen would use a biblical phrase to illustrate the theme of a song. 'Help me roll away the stone' alludes either to the boulder at the entrance to Jesus's tomb or to Jacob's feat at the well in Haran. Rolling the stone off the mouth of the well was a straightforward and decisive act that set Jacob on the path to his pre-ordained destiny. He had arrived at the well alone and impoverished, as a fugitive in fear of his life. By the time he departed he was on his way to prosperity, to a place in history and a name that would redound eternally. It was all because he rolled away the stone that covered the mouth of the well, enabling a young woman to water her sheep. Cohen uses the line in *Show Me the Place*, a song about someone trying to work out how to make their own destiny come true.

Leonard Cohen said that he used biblical imagery because it came to him naturally. He saw the Bible as a collection of stories that everybody knew, which had managed over time to maintain their hold on the popular imagination, even in the face of cultural change. He felt it important to have a common reservoir to tap into. 'Our Bible was written during one of the great periods of the language, and most of the orators of recent memory – Jesse Jackson or Martin Luther King Jr., for instance – are based in that tradition. That's where the richness of our language resides.'[2]

The Bible is, I guess, the most important book in my life ... it was the English Bible, that language, that touched me, those concerns for the way the voice is raised for instance in the songs of lamentations, the sense of grandeur in the prophets, the sense of chaotic revelation in the book of Revelation. Those kinds of modes of speech, where the heart is beating fast, there is no other book that has that scope.[3]

Leonard Cohen had a personal relationship with the Bible. It took him out of his day-to-day life and opened a window for him onto eternity; it showed him how things were going to be. In his dark, dystopian yet somehow playful song *The Future* he warned of catastrophes, disasters and misfortunes that were about to engulf the world. His foresight came about, he explained, because 'I'm the little Jew who wrote the Bible.'

STORY OF ISAAC
Songs from a Room (1969)

> **The door it opened slowly,**
> **my father he came in,**
> **I was nine years old.**
> **....**
> **He said, 'I've had a vision**
> **and you know I'm strong and holy,**
> **I must do what I've been told.'**

Few pieces of literature evoke such strong passions as the binding of Isaac. Arguably the most troubling story in the entire Hebrew Bible, the narrative is simple, the tension palpable and the dénouement puzzling. It is a classic of religious literature, yet it seems to undermine the very notion of faith in a benevolent deity.

The background to the story is God's promise to Abraham that he will be the progenitor of a great nation. Yet he is 100 years old, his wife Sarah is 90 and they still do not have children. Abraham has a son, Ishmael, the child of his concubine Hagar. But, for reasons that the Bible fails to spell out clearly, although Ishmael's descendants will also become a powerful nation, it is not through him that God's promise to Abraham will be realized.

Suddenly, miraculously, three angels appear to Abraham. They tell him that Sarah will give birth this time next year. Sarah is sceptical; she is far too old; she laughs when she hears the news. But Abraham is doggedly faithful. He holds his peace, saying nothing, waiting to see if the prophecy will come true. He has heard this promise before; nothing yet has come of it.

This time it's different. The promise is finally made real. At the allotted time, one year after the angels' visit, Sarah gives birth to a son. They call him Isaac, the word coming from a Hebrew root meaning laughter, because, Sarah says, 'God made me laugh.'

So much for the background. A few years later God appears once more to Abraham. This time the Bible introduces the story with the words 'God tested Abraham'. This should give us a clue as to what might be going on, but the idea of the test is soon forgotten, and we are quickly caught up in the drama of the narrative.[4]

'Abraham, Abraham,' calls God. '*Hineni* – here I am,' comes Abraham's reply. The Hebrew word *hineni* is used rarely in the Bible as a response to a call, but when it is used it is invariably at a moment of high drama. It is a word that Leonard Cohen will make his own in his final years, one from which he will wring every last drop of emotion.

The Bible is not extravagant in its language, yet God's instruction to Abraham is surprisingly convoluted: 'Take your son,' God says, 'your only one, the one you love, Isaac, and get yourself to the Land of Moriah, and raise him up as an offering on one of the mountains that I will show you.'

That's it. Convoluted it may be, but the impact is in no way diminished. In one sentence the divine promise is overturned. Isaac will not become a great nation. His ashes will lie on a cold altar in a faraway land, in an unknown place never before mentioned in the Bible, on an anonymous mountain, the location of which Abraham is not told.

Abraham doesn't argue. On the contrary, he gets up early the next morning, saddles his donkey, takes his two servants and Isaac, chops wood for the fire and sets off for the place where God has commanded him to go. On the third day he 'lifts up his eyes and sees the place from afar'. Telling the servants to stay where they are, he places the bundle of firewood on Isaac's shoulders and gathers up the knife and the flame from which he will kindle the fire. The two of them set off together.

Isaac is dubious. 'Here is the wood and the fire', he says, 'but where is the lamb for the offering?' Abraham replies: 'God will see for himself the lamb for the offering, my son.' The Hebrew punctuation places a slight pause before the words 'my son'. Again we are told the two of them walk together.

When they reach the appointed place, Abraham builds an altar, arranges the wood, ties Isaac up and places him on the altar, atop the wood. He stretches out his hand and takes the knife to slaughter his son. The Hebrew verbs come in a staccato burst, six in a single sentence.

Immediately, an angel calls to him, from heaven:

'Abraham, Abraham!'
'Hineni – here I am,' replies Abraham, once again.
'Don't stretch out your hand to the boy and don't do
    anything', cries the angel urgently. 'For now I know that
    you are God-fearing and you did not withhold your son
    from me.'

In a rush of anti-climax the drama is over. Almost. Abraham sees a ram caught by its horn in the bush. He sacrifices it instead of his son, and goes back down the mountain. Alone. The Bible does not say that Isaac is with him. Having twice made a point of telling us that Isaac and Abraham walked together as they ascended the mountain, the Bible doesn't mention Isaac on the way down.

And that is the end of the story. We are left on a cliff edge. Where is Isaac?

Generations of artists, musicians and writers have incorporated the Binding of Isaac in their work. Bob Dylan memorably paraphrased it:

God said to Abraham, 'Kill me a son.'
Abe said, 'Man, you must be putting me on.'
God said, 'No.'
Abe said, 'What?'
God said, 'You can do what you want, Abe, but
The next time you see me coming you better run.'
Well Abe says, 'Where you want this killing done?'
God says, 'Out on Highway 61'.

Although in his early career Dylan was the protest singer of choice, it was Leonard Cohen, not Dylan, who would turn the Binding of Isaac into a song of dissent.

Cohen's Isaac is nine years old. The ancient Jewish commentaries compute his age differently. They note that Isaac's mother, Sarah, is not mentioned in the story and they surmise, with good reason, that Abraham had not told her he was about to kill their son. They assume he took him away without her knowledge.

They also know that Sarah's death is recorded in the chapter of Genesis immediately following Abraham's near slaughter of Isaac. Clearly, they deduce, she died of shock when she heard, after the event, what her deranged, religious fanatic of a husband had nearly done to the miraculous child of her old age, her only son.

Sarah's age at her death is given as 127. She was 90 when Isaac was born. Therefore, the Talmudic rabbis deduce, Isaac was 37 years old when he and Abraham walked together up the mountain.

Treating Isaac as a grown man when the incident took place enables rabbinic tradition to read new ideas into the text. He must have been a willing participant, the tradition assumes; otherwise his father, 100 years older than him, could never have duped him into going. Isaac's willingness to submit himself to sacrifice opens up theological questions of martyrdom and salvation; it leads to a far more comfortable analysis of the story than the thought of Abraham escorting a young child to his death.

The twelfth-century Spanish rationalist commentator Abraham Ibn Ezra does not accept that Isaac was 37. Nor does he accept an alternative view that the boy was five. Ibn Ezra points out that if he had been 37, fully cognizant of what was going on, the whole episode would have been presented as a test of Isaac, not of Abraham. Equally, he couldn't have been five, because a five-year-old couldn't have carried the wood up the mountain. Ibn Ezra deduces that Isaac was probably around 13, not so different from Leonard Cohen's common-sense estimate that the child was nine.

Unlike the biblical account, Cohen's story is told from Isaac's perspective. In contrast to biblical characters, those distant, righteous people whose emotions are rarely disclosed, we can relate to Cohen's personalities, their humanity, frailty and cruelty. '**And he stood so tall above me, his blue eyes they were shining and his voice was very cold**.'

Significantly, Isaac's father, who is not named in Cohen's song, has blue eyes. Abraham was born, the Bible says, in Chaldea, now part of modern Iraq. He would have been dark-skinned, probably brown-eyed and small. Isaac's father in Cohen's song is not Abraham. He is a tall, blue-eyed Caucasian. Cohen is not telling a Bible story. He is, we will see, singing of needless sacrifice.

We have already heard that the Isaac in Cohen's story, about to be slaughtered by his father, is nine years old. Leonard Cohen was nine years old when his father died. Like the Bible, Cohen begins his song cautiously, the trauma of what is to ensue slowly unfolding at a pace less likely to traumatize the participants, or indeed us. 'Take your son, your only one, the one you love, Isaac,' says God to Abraham. According to the midrashic tradition, the tradition with which Cohen was familiar, and which his grandfather Rabbi Solomon Klonitzky-Kline cited in his book of rabbinic interpretations, this convoluted instruction was not blasted out in one breath.[5] In the biblical account we hear one side of a conversation, the responses to which are not disclosed. But the Talmud filled in the blanks:

'Take your son,' says God.
'I have two sons,' says Abraham.
'Your only son.'
'They are each only sons, Ishmael the only son of Hagar;
    Isaac, Sarah's sole child.'
'The one you love.'
'I love them both.'
'Isaac!'

'Why,' asks Rabbi Yohanan, in the Talmud, 'did God introduce the command in such a long-winded manner? Answer: So as not to freak Abraham out.'[6]

Just as the murderous command is broken gently to Abraham, so Cohen has Isaac gradually come to the realization that something is wrong. The door opens slowly as his father comes in, his eyes shining with the fire of zealotry, his voice cold as his words force the unhappy parent to face up to becoming the man his God has commanded him to be.

Cohen's anti-hero replicates Abraham's urgent inerrancy; once he has been given the command there is no holding him back. In the Bible we read: '"Offer him up on one of the mountains that I will show you." And Abraham got up early in the morning and saddled his ass.' In Cohen's *Story of Isaac* we hear '**I must do what I've been told. So he started up**

the mountain.' Zealots, whether in biblical times or today, do not need to hesitate.

Twice, as Abraham and Isaac journey, the Bible declares that the 'two of them walked together'. The repetition of the phrase reinforces the sense of intimacy, father and son walking together for a common purpose. But Leonard Cohen's wretches know no common purpose, no walking together. '**He started up the mountain, I was running, he was walking …**' The image, well known from our early years, is of a child trying to keep up with an adult. There is no togetherness in Cohen's rendition. We are leaving the Bible behind.

'**… and his axe was made of gold**.' One of the notable features of Leonard Cohen's religious symbolism is his disdain for cultural boundaries. Born a Jew and always conscious of his Jewish identity, he grew up in Christian Canada, spent many years learning with a Zen master, lived in a Buddhist monastery and became a monk. Conscious of several faiths, Cohen's lyrics weave traditions and cultures together. But it can be a fool's errand to try to identify the sources of everything he writes; much that sounds mythical could just as easily come from inside his own head. The axe of gold that Isaac's nameless, blue-eyed father carries is one such item. It is certainly not biblical. It may allude to something from a long-forgotten, distant culture. Or it may just be a vivid poetic image.

We might reasonably assume that golden axes crop up all the time in myth and legend; a golden axe is surely a symbol mysterious enough to be adopted by myth-makers. But in fact golden hatchets rarely occur in mythology and folklore. In ancient Lydia, the land where Troy and Ephesus are sited, a double-headed axe was a royal symbol, but it was not golden and it had two heads rather than being the conventional single-headed type that we presume Isaac's father carried. The Assyrians, whose empire dominated the biblical world before the rise of Babylon, required their magicians to touch a sacred tamarisk tree with a golden axe before chopping it down to make magical images. But it is unlikely that Cohen is drawing on this legend in his *Story of Isaac*; it just doesn't fit.

If the axe of gold is anything more than an image dreamed up by Cohen, its source may lie in one of Aesop's fables. The fable found its way into Korean folklore and may have been recounted on Mount Baldy, the Buddhist monastery where Cohen studied. It is a morality tale, of a poor woodcutter whose axe falls into a lake. As he bemoans his bad fortune, the spirit of the lake pokes its head out of the water. Hearing of the woodchopper's plight, the spirit dives back into the lake, re-emerging a moment later with two axes, one of gold and one of silver. 'Which is yours?' the spirit demands. 'Neither,' says the woodcutter. 'Mine was made of rusty old iron.' The spirit is so impressed with the woodcutter's honesty that he gives him all three axes: the rusty one, the silver one and the gold.

Word soon spreads of the woodcutter's good fortune, and reaches the ears of another forester. He decides to go to the lake, where he would surely receive an axe of gold. He throws his old rusty one into the water and waits for the spirit, who, sure enough, soon emerges, bearing a silver axe and one of gold. 'Which one is yours?' the spirit asks. 'The gold one!' he proclaims. 'Liar!' says the spirit, 'not only will you not receive this axe, you will not get your old one back either.'

Might Isaac's father be the wicked forester, the man who symbolizes greed and dishonesty? The man so tainted by the materialist struggles of worldly warfare that he is willing even to sacrifice his own son? Or is the axe of gold simply the product of Cohen's imagination?

True to its nature, the axe of gold splits Cohen's narrative in two. It marks the moment at which he moves away from the biblical account of Isaac's sacrifice and turns instead to the crucifixion. A connection between the two narratives has long been recognized; motifs from the Isaac story surface at various places in the Gospels. They include the place where Isaac was nearly sacrificed, the motif of the lamb and the cross that Jesus carried through the streets of Jerusalem.

Mount Moriah, where Abraham was told to sacrifice Isaac, is associated in Jewish tradition with Jerusalem. Jerusalem, of course, was the site of the crucifixion. Both Abraham and Jesus arrive at Jerusalem on a donkey. Abraham is accompanied by two servants; Jesus is escorted by two disciples.

Isaac asks Abraham, 'Where is the lamb for the sacrifice?' Abraham hints that Isaac himself is the lamb, the Hebrew word for 'lamb' sounding a little like the Greek for 'you'. The early rabbinic interpretations were composed by people who knew both Hebrew and Greek. They would have understood the pun, appreciating that 'The lamb for the sacrifice my son' could also be read as 'You are the sacrifice my son'. When understood in this way, Isaac is equated with a sacrificial lamb. Jesus, of course, is the lamb of God.

Jesus, according to the Gospel of John, carries his cross, the instrument of his execution, just as Isaac carries the wood on which he will be incinerated. As long ago as the third century an anonymous Jewish commentator recognized the similarities between the two narratives. In his exposition of the verse 'Abraham took the wood for the burnt offering and put it on his son Isaac', the commentator declared, 'like one who carries his cross upon his shoulder'.[7]

But in Cohen's song Isaac does not carry the wood on his shoulder. Unlike the account in Genesis, his father has not brought the wood with him from home. That's why he is carrying an axe. We have moved away from Genesis. We reach the crucifixion in the next verse.

Then my father built an altar,
He looked once behind his shoulder,
He knew I would not hide.

To reach the site where the altar was to be built, Isaac and his father had to climb the mountain. Genesis, in its matter-of-fact account, does not describe the view as they ascended. Cohen, in his Isaac-centred parable, does. The trees grow smaller as they climb; the lake shrinks to the size of a lady's mirror. In his account the boy and his father stop during their ascent of the mountain to drink some wine. His father throws the empty bottle away; it breaks. It is Cohen's reference to the wine that leads us to the crucifixion.

At the Last Supper, Jesus takes the cup of wine and tells his disciples to drink from it, for it is his blood of the covenant. The covenant, as the Gospel of Mark makes clear, is a new covenant, echoing that foretold by the prophet Jeremiah in the Hebrew Bible. It is to supersede the covenant made between God and Israel at Mount Sinai, when Moses sacrificed bullocks and sprinkled their blood on the people, declaring it 'the blood of the covenant'. The new covenant that Jesus ordains is to be established in his blood, on the cross, and symbolized by the wine in his cup. He tells his disciples he will not drink from the fruit of the vine again until the kingdom of God comes.

There is no mention of wine in Genesis, which is unconcerned with the food and drink that Isaac and Abraham consume on their journey up the mountain. So when Cohen has Isaac and his nameless father pause for wine, in their ascent up the mountain, he must be thinking not of Genesis but of the Gospels. They are drinking the wine of the Last Supper, the wine that symbolizes Jesus' blood, the wine of Holy Communion. And here is the twist in Cohen's tale. For, having drunk the communion wine, Isaac's father discards the bottle, throwing it some way off. The act of communion is shattered when Isaac's father chucks the bottle away, breaking it.

The story grows darker. In Christianity the crucifixion is the prelude to the resurrection. In Jewish tradition Isaac's near-slaughter on the altar is understood as a redemptive act. Isaac, we recall, did not come down from the mountain with his father. He doesn't reappear in Genesis for several chapters. Several old Jewish legends try to explain where he has been, a few even hinting that he was indeed slaughtered but revived. But Cohen's nine-year-old victim will neither be resurrected like Jesus nor revived like the biblical Isaac. His father has thrown away the blood of the covenant, the wine of the communion. The bottle is broken. There is no happy ending to this story.

Two more biblical images in Cohen's song demand our attention. As he climbed with his father, Cohen's Isaac thought he might have seen an eagle. He wasn't certain; it might have been a vulture. A special place is reserved in the Bible for the eagle, the king of the birds. An eagle is one of the four faces of the angelic creatures in the heavenly retinue, described in the first chapter of Ezekiel. Eagles are compassionate, and protective. In Deuteronomy the eagle 'flutters over its young, it spreads its wings and takes him, it bears him on his pinions'. When the Israelites left Egypt, they were, says Exodus, borne aloft on eagles' wings.

Isaac sees an eagle, a symbol of divine protection, and his heart lifts. Or is it a vulture, circling for carrion? Cohen's Isaac does not yet know how this story will end.

As for his father, he built his altar. As Abraham did. He looked behind him. As Abraham did. But Abraham did not look behind him until he had been told not to slaughter his son. When he did look, he saw a ram caught by its horn in a bush. Waiting to be sacrificed in place of the biblical Isaac whose life has now been saved.

But Cohen's Isaac will not be saved. '**He knew I would not hide**.' There is no trapped ram to substitute for this Isaac. The story did not end well.

First recorded in 1969, at a time of mass protest against the Vietnam War, *Story of Isaac* is not a Bible story. It is Bible as metaphor. As Leonard Cohen told his East Berlin audience in 1972, immortalized in his *Live Songs* album the following year: 'It's about those who would sacrifice one generation on behalf of another.'

The sacrifice is not always in war.

I was careful in that song to try and put it beyond the pure, beyond the simple, anti-war protest ... it isn't necessarily for war that we're willing to sacrifice each other. We'll get some idea – some magnificent idea – that we're willing to sacrifice each other for; it doesn't necessarily have to involve an opponent or an ideology, but human beings, being what they are, we're always going to set up people to die for some absurd situation that we define as important.[8]

THE BUTCHER
Songs from a Room (1969)

The Butcher appears on *Songs from a Room,* the same album as *Story of Isaac*. It too discusses ideas of human sacrifice and the slaughter of innocents, the story beginning this time with the crucifixion. The album was released in 1969, at a time when Cohen's tormented life was in even greater turmoil than usual; there is a dark spirituality to several of the tracks.

Cohen was approaching his 35th birthday when *Songs from a Room* was issued. He had been living on the Greek island of Hydra on and off since 1960, most of the time with his first great love, Marianne Ihlen, and her young son Axel. Hydra – with its steep, narrow lanes free from traffic, white-terraced, red-roofed cottages, picturesque harbour and lazy, unhurried bars – was home to a small community of artists and writers, mainly English-speakers. It offered a serene existence to those who yearned for nothing more than peaceful, sun-soaked, island tranquillity in a closely knit colony of expats.

Cohen's life with Marianne in their Hydra home was idyllic in many ways. But economic demands, career ambitions and his innate, ethnic restlessness meant that there were always reasons why he needed to leave, to return to Canada and the USA, sometimes for months at a time. He lived on Hydra with Marianne for eight years, generally for about six months of each year. 'Then the other six months I was stuck somewhere else. Then I found I was living with her four months of the year, then two months of the year and then about the eighth year I was living with her a couple of weeks of the year.'[9]

Eventually Cohen suggested that Marianne join him in New York. He rented a loft for her and Axel on the Lower East Side but didn't move in with them. He remained in his room in the chaotic Chelsea Hotel, home over the decades to dozens of artists, writers and musicians, and he had other women in his life apart from Marianne. His famous song *So Long, Marianne*, on his 1967 album *Songs of Leonard Cohen*, was recorded as their relationship was winding down, a slow and protracted break-up. Marianne's picture appears on the back cover of *Songs from a Room*, sitting at a desk in their Hydra living room, in front of Cohen's Olivetti typewriter.

Leonard Cohen once said that *The Butcher* had a psychic integrity:

You could dignify it with a religious interpretation. I'm not interested in that, if people want to do that. If they want to dignify it or elaborate it on altars or dissecting tables or whatever it is – it's cool with me. Everybody's job should be protected. To me, when the energy is somehow generated within somebody to create something, the thing has to stand or fall by its own internal construction. To me that's another little song that has an internal authenticity or accuracy that allows it to exist.[10]

He was adamant that *The Butcher* need not have a religious interpretation. Nevertheless, he filled it with religious symbolism. The lamb, the butcher and the person telling the story are all introduced as if they are biblical characters. This does not, of course, make it a religious song.

The song begins with the narrator encountering a butcher who is slaughtering a lamb. He accuses the butcher of torturing the animal, but the slaughterer is not deterred. '**Listen to me, child**,' says the butcher in response to the accusation: '**I am what I am, and you, you are my only son**.' It's only one line in the song, but the biblical imagery could not be more powerful; and there couldn't be a greater contrast between the two images that the line evokes.

'**I am what I am**' comes from the book of Exodus. Moses, who had run away from Egypt to escape Pharaoh's wrath, was in the wilderness, shepherding his father-in-law's sheep. He saw a bush in flame. A voice called to him from the bush, telling him to return to Egypt and liberate the Israelites from slavery.

Moses was not happy with what he had just heard. He protested that he was not the right man for the job, but God, for his was the voice, was insistent. As Moses began to realize that he had no option but to obey, he asked what he was supposed to say when the Israelites demanded proof that he really was on a divine mission. 'When I say to them "The God of your ancestors sent me to you," and they ask me "What is his name?" What shall I say to them?' God replied: 'I am what I am.' He continued: 'This is what you will say to the Children of Israel: I am has sent me to you.'[11]

'I am what I am' is the name of the God who spoke to Moses. '**I am what I am**' is the name of the butcher, responding to the narrator who accused him as he slaughtered the lamb. God, it appears, has been cast in the role of the butcher.

Having made himself known, the butcher then declared: '**You are my only son**.' The 'only son' is how Jesus is described in the Gospel of John: 'the one and only Son, who came from the Father'.[12] God the butcher is addressing Jesus the only son.

But this gives us a problem. The way that Cohen has written his lyric implies that the butcher is talking to the narrator. In other words that the butcher is '**I am what I am**' and the narrator is Jesus, the '**only son**'. But if we leave the dialogue aside and just consider the three characters in the scene, the one most likely to be Jesus is not the narrator but the lamb. Jesus is the 'Lamb of God', according to both the Gospel of John and the book of Revelation. Cohen frequently made use of Revelation in his music and poetry.

Jesus is called a lamb because he was sacrificed. The earliest New Testament reference to the lamb of God is in Paul's First Letter to the Corinthians, where Jesus is called 'Our Passover Lamb'. The phrase links Jesus' crucifixion to the Passover, when the Israelites were told to kill, roast and eat a lamb before being liberated from Egypt.

In Jesus' time Jews celebrated Passover in Jerusalem with a festive meal, the centrepiece of which was the Passover sacrifice, a roasted lamb. A condition of the meal was that it was to be eaten in groups; nobody was to eat it alone. Some people ate with their families, some with their friends. Some ate it with their disciples. According to the Gospels, the Last

Supper was a festive Passover meal, Jesus and the disciples eating together in a group.[13] And although the Bible is silent on whether or not they ate a lamb at the meal, since it was a Passover meal, the lamb was there symbolically, even if not physically.

Jesus was taken from his Passover meal to be crucified. He was sacrificed like a Passover lamb. So, when the butcher says '**you are my only son**', we should probably assume that he has turned away from the narrator and is addressing the lamb that he is slaughtering. The reason starts to become clear in the second verse.

> **Well, I found a silver needle,**
> **I put it into my arm.**

If Leonard Cohen hadn't written this verse, we might have assumed that the whole song is about the crucifixion. But in this second verse the scene has changed dramatically. We are no longer in the Bible. Some people have argued that the silver needle the singer puts into his arm represents the nails on the cross, but it is unlikely; there is nothing in the rest of the verse to back up such a suggestion. Rather, Cohen is singing about the world we live in, about a drug user who, as the rest of the verse makes clear, is struggling to get through the night. The silver needle, he says, did some good, but it also did some harm, and the verse ends with him wondering why the night was so long. We all know that feeling.

It took more than 30 years for Cohen to give us a hint about what was going on in this song. It came in his song *Amen*, on his 2012 *Old Ideas* album. It's a song in which he challenges God about the injustices of the world, and particularly about the Holocaust:

> **Tell me again**
> **When the filth of the butcher**
> **Is washed in the blood of the lamb ...**
> **When the rest of the culture**
> **Has passed thru' the Eye of the Camp.**

The 'blood of the lamb' is a phrase from the New Testament's book of Revelation. It refers to a born-again multitude who have 'washed their robes, and made them white in the blood of the Lamb'.[14] The blood of the lamb, Revelation tells us, purifies; it is the blood of the crucified Jesus. The blood of the lamb, says Cohen in *Amen*, will wash away the filth of the butcher who, we now see is responsible for the Holocaust, for herding the culture, the slaughtered victims, through the gates of the camp.

So the butcher turns out to be the murderer at the Holocaust (whether one man or the entire Nazi gang is of little consequence to the song). Returning to *The Butcher's* first verse, we can now see that, rather than singing of the crucifixion, of God sacrificing his son for the sake of religion and salvation, Cohen is singing of something far darker. Comparing the Holocaust to the crucifixion, he has cast Jesus, the '**only son**', in the role of victim and has placed God, '**I am what I am**', in the role of the murderers: the camp guards or the SS or the entire Nazi machinery.

The song, we begin to see, is a condemnation of whatever divine plan led to the slaughter of innocents, exemplified by the Nazi Holocaust but taking in many other injustices throughout history as well. To drive home his point, Cohen begins his next verse with passing optimism, before twisting the knife in his final confrontation with the butcher, forcing him onto the defensive.

The third verse begins with the drug-taking narrator seeing flowers grow at the very spot where the lamb fell. It is a positive, cheerful image, evoking hope, banishing despair. The placing of flowers on a coffin, at a grave or by the roadside symbolizes not only memory and love; it declares the triumph of life over death.

Cohen may have been inspired to use a flower metaphor by the work of his great literary hero, the Spanish revolutionary poet Federico García Lorca. In his poems Lorca treats flowers as a symbol of healing and hope; he writes of 'having no flower, pulp or clay for the worm of my despair', and of the nun who embroiders flowers for an altar cloth for the five wounds of Christ.[15]

Unsurprisingly, flowers are also associated with certain Christian resurrection traditions. In the Easter ritual of Flowering the Cross, which marks the transition from Good Friday to Easter Sunday, from crucifixion to resurrection, worshippers decorate a wooden cross with flowers. It is an optimism similar to Cohen's when he sees flowers growing where the lamb fell. The anger he felt, when he first accused the butcher of torturing the lamb, is transmuting into hope. Death, he now sees, is followed by resurrection; despair looks as if it will give way to a bright, optimistic future. The Holocaust should be followed by the optimism of a new future, a new Israel arising from the ashes of the old.

But he knows it will not be that simple. Life is not so straightforward. Now he sees things with a new clarity. He rails against the underlying premise of the scene he imagines he is witnessing. The crucifixion is based on an idea first posited when Abraham took Isaac up the mountain, that sacrifice leads to redemption, that there is such a thing as sacred, redemptive slaughter. He sees the flowers growing, realizes that there will be a resurrection, but he is not impressed. '**Was I supposed to praise my Lord, make some kind of joyful sound?**' he demands in the continuation of the verse. Am I to praise God for the resurrection, demands Cohen? Praise him for the end of the slaughter, for the defeat of the Nazis, the victory of the forces of good over the forces of evil? Surely celebrating the resurrection of the slain lamb lets the butcher off the hook; the murder should never have happened in the first place. What is he praising God for? The slaughter should not have occurred.

Now the song changes. Now God becomes the one in despair. He begs Cohen to listen to him. '**Listen, listen to me now, I go round and round**.' As God, he tells Cohen, he is caught up in the never-ending spiral of divine existence, whatever that might mean, however we may conceive it. '**You,**' however, he says to Cohen, '**are my only child. Do**

not leave me now.' In a moment of astonishing pathos, God declares his dependence on humanity.

In the end it is Cohen who is vindicated. He started the song accusing the butcher; now, as his ode draws to a close, he sees that the accusation has had an effect. As the song ends, God declares that he has fallen, is wounded. He says there is blood on his body, ice on his soul. '**Lead on, my son**,' he concludes. '**It is your world**.'

God has handed Cohen the reins, has renounced to him his divine mastery of the cosmos. All it needed, it seems, was for Cohen to refuse to give thanks for the sacrifice, to not make the 'kind of joyful sound' that was expected of him. God cannot rule if he is not acknowledged by his creation. If humanity will not validate him, he will become powerless, and the world will proceed under its own steam.

Cohen had said that *The Butcher* did not need a religious interpretation, that it had to stand or fall on its own merits. It is internally rigorous, the story of a man who on hearing of, or even surviving, the Holocaust tries to understand it in terms of the crucifixion. He turns to drugs, but he is so steeped in his own anger, in his own drug-fuelled indignation, that even when he visualizes flowers growing at the site of the crucifixion he refuses to be optimistic. He will not praise God for ameliorating an act that need not, that should not, have happened at all.

And God concurs. Trapped in the revolving seasons of his own creation, he accepts that if he is not to be praised, he can no longer be in control of the world.

The Butcher is not a poem of salvation through martyrdom. The clue is in the title. '**Butcher**' is not a word one would normally use to signify someone carrying out a sacrificial act. Rather, the song is a protest against the doctrine of salvation, against the foundational narrative of both Christianity and Judaism, that sacrifice leads to redemption, that good can come out of evil. For, as we saw in *Story of Isaac*, the crucifixion of Jesus and the near-sacrifice of Isaac are, in essence, one and the same thing.

Arguably, *The Butcher* had to be written by a Jew. Arguing with God, challenging him, even accusing him, is what Jews do. Whether it's Abraham protesting against the impending destruction of Sodom and Gomorrah, Tevye the milkman in *Fiddler on the Roof* asking what possible difference it could make if he were a rich man or the rabbis in Auschwitz putting God on trial for breaking his covenant with the Jews, Jews have a tradition of challenging God. And in *The Butcher*, as he will do 30 years later in *Amen*, Cohen holds fast to that tradition.

HALLELUJAH
Various Positions (1984)

Now I've heard there was a secret chord
That David played, and it pleased the Lord ...

Leonard Cohen described *Hallelujah* as a song about a
conflicted world, in which there are things that cannot be
reconciled. Nevertheless, 'regardless of what the impossibility
of the situation is, there is a moment when you open your
mouth and you throw open your arms ... and you just say
"Hallelujah!"'[16]

Far and away his most famous song, recorded by over 300
artists, *Hallelujah* took Cohen five years to write, during
which he composed and discarded dozens of verses. He
recorded it in 1984, on his album *Various Positions*, but the
song didn't really have much of an impact until Jeff Buckley
released a version ten years later. Then, in 2008, Alexandra
Burke's gospel version won the ITV talent show *The X Factor*,
and her record shot to number one in the UK charts. Jeff
Buckley's version was immediately reissued, displacing the
Burke version at the top, and Cohen's original 1984 recording
came in at number 36. So, nearly 20 years after he began
writing it, Cohen's own *Hallelujah* finally made the charts,
accompanied by two cover versions.

The opening verse of *Hallelujah* is based on a biblical story
about King David. David occupies an exalted place in Cohen's
pantheon: in a 1994 interview Cohen described him, along with

Homer, Wordsworth, Milton and Dante, as 'the embodiment of our highest possibility'.[17] There are elements of self-identification here. King David and Leonard Cohen have much in common – both consummate musicians, players of stringed instruments, accomplished lovers and garlanded poets. The one thing they don't share is royalty; David may have been a king, but Cohen knew that, as a *cohen*, a member of the priestly Hebrew tribe, he could never sit on Israel's throne. Too much power may not be concentrated in one man's hands.[18]

A shared identity, then, as musicians, lovers and poets. In *Hallelujah*, Cohen addresses each of these aspects of their shared identity in turn and draws our attention to the irreconcilable conflicts they present.

Despite a career stained by extra-judicial killing, adultery and many fierce, bloody battles, King David is described in the book of Samuel as the 'sweet singer in Israel'. He is the progenitor of the eternal royal line in Israel; his throne, Jewish tradition declares, will one day be restored for all eternity. The Messiah – may he come speedily, but not before you finish this book – will be a direct descendant of David. The gospels of Matthew and Luke both trace Jesus' lineage through the male line back to David.

David is a complex and contradictory character. He makes his entrance onto the biblical stage when Saul, Israel's first king, begins to exhibit signs of instability. God tells the prophet Samuel, the nation's spiritual leader, to secretly anoint David, a Bethlehem shepherd, the youngest of Jesse's eight sons, as Saul's successor. But Samuel is not to depose Saul yet.[19]

Shortly after this, Saul suffers a breakdown. He was never really cut out for leadership; he could not cope with the pressures of being king. His servants, believing he is troubled by an evil spirit, suggest that he get himself a musician, to play to him and soothe his nerves. One of his attendants tells him of a shepherd he has seen in Bethlehem, 'a musician, a mighty soldier, a man of war, intelligent, good looking and God is with him'. He means David.

Saul, who, with hindsight, should probably have paid more attention to the 'mighty soldier, man of war' bit, is enraptured by David's musical prowess, his charm and his good looks. David plucks his harp, Saul listens, and his terror of the evil spirit departs.

David joined Saul's court, killed Goliath and became best friends with the king's son Jonathan. The women loved the young, handsome warrior–musician David, they sang songs in his praise, and Saul grew increasingly jealous. Eventually David felt he had no choice but to flee the court. He lived for some years as a rebel chieftain with a band of followers. Adventure followed adventure until Saul and Jonathan were both killed in battle by the Philistines, Israel's long-standing enemy to the south. David emerged from hiding, the people acclaimed him and his destiny was fulfilled. He became king.

This is the biblical background to Cohen's song. It all took place before David played the secret chord.

A legend in the Talmud describes how, when he was king, David would wake up at midnight to play his harp. There is no mention of this in the Bible, but the legend crops up in several early Jewish sources.[20] When they heard David play, all the sages in his kingdom would arise and gather together to study God's word. It is this secret chord that David played which '**pleased the Lord**' in the opening stanza of Cohen's *Hallelujah*.

In another version of the legend the north wind blew each midnight, plucking the strings of a harp hanging at the head of David's bed. As soon as he heard the chord, David awoke to study. When Satan, the angel of temptation, asked David why he didn't indulge himself by lying in bed until mid-morning, as kings were apparently supposed to do, he replied that his honour was nothing compared with that of his Creator. It was his duty to arise and study the divine law. No wonder the Lord was pleased.

None of this is in the Bible. The only important mention of David's harp playing is when he is first summoned to play for Saul, to ease his terror of the evil spirit that plagues him. The legends that Cohen draws upon for his song are all in the ancient folklore tradition that expands and elaborates on the biblical text, providing us with the story behind the story.

The Hebrew word *Hallelujah* means 'praise God'. It occurs only in the book of Psalms and indeed appears in only 15 of that book's 150 odes. So, although it is very familiar, cropping up over and again in both Christian and Jewish liturgy, *Hallelujah* is, biblically speaking, quite an unusual word. It's one of very few words in the Hebrew language made up of two words run together. Strictly speaking we should translate it as one word: 'PraiseGod'.

David's career as king was marked by warfare, strife and intrigue. But he never lost his affinity for poetry and music. He wrote many psalms. Several are attributed to him, and the book of Psalms, roughly half-way through, declares: 'Here end the Psalms of David son of Jesse.' But he did not write the word *Hallelujah*. All 15 psalms containing the word *Hallelujah* occur in the second half of the book, after we have read that the psalms of David have concluded. Yet, although the book of Psalms itself does not consider David to have written the word *Hallelujah*, the religious tradition disagrees. The Talmud declares that David wrote all the psalms, even those that clearly refer to events after his time. When Leonard Cohen writes about David composing 'Hallelujah', he is drawing on the Talmudic tradition.[21]

As a musician David is painfully aware, despite God's many ethical and legal commands, that there is no religious injunction to play or sing music. Shakespeare's 'If music be the food of love' seems to have little place in the early biblical narratives; there are only a handful of songs in the Bible before David came along with his psalms. God, it would appear, in biblical times was not partial to being worshipped through music. Hence the words that Cohen puts into David's mouth: **'But you don't really care for music, do you?'**

David, urged on by his musical spirit, is baffled. He knows that his secret chord pleases the Lord, yet he can find no evidence in the Israelite tradition that music is the medium through which his God wishes to be worshipped ... **'The baffled king composing Hallelujah'**.

Cohen draws on another Talmudic legend for his second verse:

Your faith was strong but you needed proof.
You saw her bathing on the roof.

The setting is the episode of David and Bathsheba, the occasion of David's most egregious offence, as a result of which he suffers calamity upon calamity.[22] Constantly at war, David had sent his troops to besiege the city of Rabbah, capital of the neighbouring tribe of Ammon. He remained behind, attending to affairs of state in his Jerusalem palace. Finding the heat of the autumn evening oppressive, David went up to his roof and gazed out over the city. From his vantage point he saw a woman bathing. He could see her beauty even from the distance of his roof. He asked his servants who she was; they told him that she was Bathsheba, the wife of Uriah the Hittite. Unconcerned that she was a married woman, David sent for her and slept with her. The Bible does not give us any detail of the seduction, if that is what it was, and we do not know her feelings on the matter. A few weeks later she sent a message to David telling him she was pregnant.

Unwilling to disclose his adultery to the world, David recalled her husband from his service at the siege. The king's excuse was that he wanted to find out how the troops were faring. His real reason, however, was to have Uriah go back home to spend some time with his wife, so that when the baby was born he would assume that it was his. But Uriah did not go home. He remained in the palace, in the servants' quarters. He told David that he could not possibly go back to his wife and enjoy himself while his comrades were still at war.

Unable to extricate himself from this dilemma, David compounded his sin by telling Uriah's commander to send him into the front line of battle, knowing that he would almost certainly be killed. With Uriah dead, Bathsheba will be a free woman, able to sleep with whomever she likes. Sure enough, Uriah is killed and David takes Bathsheba into his harem. It is not until the prophet Nathan rebukes him, informing him that he has brought disaster upon himself and his household, that David begins to comprehend the magnitude of what he has done.

This is the background to Cohen's line '**You saw her bathing on the roof**'. But it is the preceding line that should interest us: '**Your faith was strong but you needed proof.**' The Bible makes no mention of David's faith in this story, or of his need for proof. But the Talmud does. Like many Talmudic legends, the story it tells has no historical basis; this legend is an allegory on the dangers of hubris. David, in the Talmud's story, has asked God why, when Jews pray, they speak of the God of Abraham, Isaac and Jacob, but never the God of David. God explains that he had tested the patriarchs Abraham, Isaac and Jacob and that they had proved themselves to be upstanding and worthy. David asks God to test him so that he may prove himself. God, knowing that David cannot control his sexual desire, says that he will test him with a married woman. David, of course, fails the test. This proves, says the Talmud, that we should never willingly subject ourselves to an ordeal that we are likely to fail.[23]

The verse continues:

She tied you to a kitchen chair
She broke your throne, and she cut your hair.

The Bible is rarely predictable. We might think that biblical morality would guarantee that David and Bathsheba's adulterous union would be cursed, that no good could possibly come of it. And on one level this turns out to be the case: David is plagued by misfortune for the rest of his life. But of all David's many children, born to several different wives, the one who wins the fraternal struggle to succeed his father on the throne is Bathsheba's son, Solomon.

Solomon, like his father, was a figure of complex ambiguity. Wise yet foolish, he consolidated the Hebrew faith by building the Jerusalem Temple, yet he accumulated wealth to excess, growing lustful in his old age, worshipping foreign gods and sowing the seeds of the nation's decline. After his death the kingdom he ruled fell apart. '**She broke your throne**.' David's eternal throne was broken due to the excesses of Solomon, the son he had with Bathsheba, the woman with whom he committed adultery, whose husband he had sent to his death in war.

One of the many catastrophes of David's reign in the years following his 'seduction' of Bathsheba was the rebellion of another of his sons, Absalom, against his father. Absalom, young, good-looking and extremely long-haired, seized power and proclaimed himself king. David, by now an old man, was forced to flee Jerusalem. But David was shrewder and more experienced than his vainglorious son. He planted agents in Absalom's camp, confounded the rebels' plans and won a decisive battle against them. As Absalom fled, his mule passed under a low-hanging terebinth tree and his hair was caught in its branches. The mule carried on, and the young pretender was left hanging, exposed to David's forces. They slew him. Absalom met his doom through his ambition and vanity: another way in which David's throne was '**broken**'.[24]

'**She cut your hair**.' Absalom's hair caused his death, but not because it had been cut. The shorn hair that Cohen sings of may allude to Absalom, but it fits Samson far better. Living several generations before David, Samson was another conflicted character who allowed his passion to overcome his reason. Samson is the strongman of the Bible, a legendary hero who scraped honey out of the belly of a lion and slew a thousand Philistines with the jawbone of an ass. His strength lay in his luxurious growth of hair. Before he was born, an angel had appeared to his mother commanding her that the hair of the son she would bear was never to be cut.

Samson lived during a period of continual skirmishes between the Israelites and their southern neighbours, the Philistines. His great strength enabled him to terrorize the enemy; they in turn were desperate to capture him. As with David, desire proved his downfall. He fell in love with Delilah, a Philistine woman, who found herself torn between loyalty to her people and her love for him. She urged him daily to reveal the source of his strength, and although he resisted, her will was stronger than his. When he finally told her that his strength was due to his uncut hair, she lulled him to sleep on her knees and handed him over to the Philistines. When he awoke, he found that his hair had gone, and consequently his strength. The Philistines chained him, threw him in the dungeon and put out his eyes. Samson's downfall, like Absalom's, came about through his hair.

The Mishnah, the third-century Jewish text which the Talmud expands, links Absalom and Samson explicitly: 'Samson went after [the desire of] his eyes; therefore the Philistines put out his eyes ... Absalom was proud of his hair, therefore he was hanged by his hair.'[25] This is the connection that Leonard Cohen is drawing on when he links David's broken throne to Delilah shearing Samson's hair. From David seeing Bathsheba bathing to Samson losing his strength, the whole verse is about the conflicts in men who find themselves unable to control their desires. Ultimately, all that is left to them is the singing of '**Hallelujah**': '**And from your tongue she drew the Hallelujah**'.

Words are both sacred and mundane. Their potency is deeply rooted in both Christian and Jewish traditions. Having dealt in his first two verses with the conflicted musician and lover, Cohen completes his ode with a meditation on the paradoxical nature of words.

> **You say I took the name in vain**
> **I don't even know the name ...**
> **There's a blaze of light in every word.**

The third of the Ten Commandments, the injunction against blasphemy, declares: 'Thou shalt not take the name of the Lord your God in vain.'[26] Several people in the Bible are charged with committing blasphemy. Among them are Jesus, who is accused by Caiaphas the High Priest, and the anonymous son of an Egyptian, who blasphemed in the wilderness. However, David is not accused of blasphemy, either in the Bible or in folklore. The closest he gets is when, after his adultery with Bathsheba, the prophet Nathan enters David's chambers to deliver an excoriating rebuke. He tells him that the sword will never depart from his house, because he has spurned God.[27]

But spurning God is not blasphemy, and Cohen's second line, '**I don't even know the name**', doesn't seem to apply to any of those accused in the Bible of blasphemy. The biblical character who doesn't know God's name is Moses, at the Burning Bush. As we saw in *The Butcher*, he asked God how he should refer to him when the Israelites asked who had sent him. Moses didn't know God's name, the Name that is not to be taken in vain.

There is no hint of blasphemy in Moses' protestations at the Burning Bush. Indeed, Moses doesn't take the Name in vain anywhere in the Bible. But a story in the Zohar, the primary text of Kabbalah, tells us otherwise. According to the Zohar, Moses did take the Name in vain, or at least made vain use of it.

The Zohar's claim comes in the course of a discussion about Moses' staff, the wondrous rod he carried with him, with which he performed his miracles. When Moses first met Pharaoh and needed to demonstrate his power, he cast his staff to the ground. Immediately it turned into a serpent. Pharaoh's magicians, not to be outdone, did the same with their staffs, but Moses' serpentine staff swallowed them all up. Later, whenever he was commanded to bring a plague on the Egyptians, Moses would wave his staff towards the heavens, whereupon the plague would descend. And, in the most demonstrative of all his miracles, when the fleeing Israelite slaves were trapped between the Red Sea in front of them and Pharaoh's army behind them, Moses stretched out his staff over the waters. The Red Sea parted, and the Israelites marched through on dry land.

But the Bible tells us that on one occasion Moses misused the staff. Towards the end of their journey through the wilderness the Israelites were complaining that they had no water. It wasn't the first time they had made this complaint. Previously God had shown Moses a rock, telling him to strike it with his staff. Moses did so, and water flowed out. Now, with the Israelites complaining again, God showed him another rock. He told Moses to take his staff, but he wasn't to do anything with it. Instead he was just to hold it in is hand while speaking to the rock. Water, he was assured, would once again gush out.

Moses was frustrated. He was an old man, and for 40 years he'd patiently put up with the Israelites' complaints. The weather was hot and, to cap it all, his sister Miriam had just died. He was in no mood to speak to rocks. He took his staff and, as he had done the previous time, he struck the rock.

Nothing happened. He struck it again. This time water came out. But God was angry. He told Moses that because had shown a lack of faith, because he had not sanctified God in the eyes of the people, he would not be allowed to enter the Promised Land.[28]

Many commentators have tried to explain why Moses was punished so severely for this error. The Zohar's explanation seems to be the one that Cohen follows. According to mystical legend, a legend that pre-dates the Zohar, Moses' staff was inscribed with the sacred, secret name of God. It was the Name which gave the staff its powers. The Zohar says that God was angry because, in smiting the rock, Moses had abused the holy Name engraved upon his staff. It quotes God as saying: 'I did not give you the staff for this purpose. By your life it will not be in your hand from this moment onward.'[29]

As a young man, at the Burning Bush, Moses had not known the Name. As an old man he took it in vain, abusing the staff on which it had been engraved. But then, in the third line of the verse, Cohen throws in a twist. Even if he had known the Name, he asks, what was it to God anyway? Names, Cohen seems to be saying, are only words. What does it matter?

Cohen's question is rhetorical. The Name mattered to Cohen, not just in *Hallelujah* but personally as well. He adhered to the Jewish religious tradition that forbids the writing out in full of God's name. Look in any of Cohen's books or lyrics copied from his hand, and you will find he nearly always writes 'G-d' instead of 'God'. Not writing God's name in full protects it against destruction should something happen to the paper on which it is written. It ensures that the Name cannot be taken in vain.

But if words are only words, why does the Name matter? In the final lines of the verse Cohen explains why. He sings of the blaze of light to be found in every word. It is this blaze of light that explains why taking the Name in vain matters. Names may be nothing more than words. Yet words are the most powerful force in existence. The world came into existence through words. In the first chapter of Genesis, God created the world through speech: 'And God said let there be light. And there was light.'[30] Or, as the Gospel of John formulates it: 'In the beginning was the Word and the Word was with God, and the Word was God.'[31]

Names are powerful because they encapsulate our essence. A Talmudic tradition recommends that if someone wishes to change their identity they should change their name.[32] A desperately sick person has their name changed through a prayer in the synagogue. Folklore says that this is so the Angel of Death can't find them, but the deeper reason is that by changing our name we change our fundamental nature.

Cohen didn't approve of name-changing. Growing up in Canada among families who had arrived not so long ago with long, unpronounceable, Eastern European surnames, Cohen knew many people who had anglicized their names. His friend Irving Layton had been born in Romania as Yisroel Lazarovitch. 'I like to see the marks on people,' Cohen said in 1980. 'I never liked the idea of people changing their names. It's just nice to know where you come from.'[33]

Words matter. In the mystical tradition of the Kabbalah, the universe was constructed from 32 building blocks: the ten utterances that God spoke at Creation plus the 22 letters of the Hebrew alphabet, the language of Creation. Words and letters, imply the Kabbalah, are sacred. Cohen agrees. Discussing his *Book of Mercy*, the collection of psalm-like poems that he published in 1984, he said: 'I always feel that the world was created through words, through speech in our tradition, and I've always seen the enormous light in charged speech, and that's what I've tried to get to.'[34] **'There's a blaze of light in every word**.'

Yet words are also mundane. We throw them around, particularly when our passions get the better of us. The irreconcilable conflict that Cohen highlights in this verse is between the sacred word and the secular, between holy and profane speech. Unable to resolve the dilemma, all we can do is open our mouths, throw up our arms and recite '**The holy or the broken Hallelujah**'.

I did my best, it wasn't much,
I couldn't feel, so I tried to touch.

In his final verse Cohen turns the spotlight on himself. He did his best, he sings, even though it wasn't much. Because he couldn't feel, he tried to touch. A perceptive article by Jiří Měsíc understands this line as a confession that because he couldn't feel the divine love he had to be satisfied with touching. Měsíc sees *Hallelujah* as sanctifying the physical act of love: '"The holy or the broken Hallelujah," meaning that God may be reached either through sacred meditation or through sex, as both lead to the union with Him'.[35] As for Cohen, all he can do is stand before the Lord '**with nothing on my tongue but Hallelujah**'.

Cohen spoke about *Hallelujah* when he played in Warsaw in 1985: 'I know that there is an eye that watches all of us. There is a judgement that weighs everything we do. And before this great force, which is greater than any government, I stand in awe and I kneel in respect. And it is to this great judgement that I dedicate this next song: *Hallelujah*.'

Three years later, though, he had rewritten the lyrics, removing the biblical references. He told his audience in Antwerp why: 'It was a song that had these references to the Bible in it, although these references became more and more remote as the song went from beginning to end. And finally I understood that it was not necessary to refer to the Bible any more. And I rewrote the song.'[36]

INTERLUDE:
LEONARD COHEN'S RELIGIOUS EDUCATION

Leonard Cohen's ability to use the Bible as a canvas on which to paint his own ideas owes a tremendous amount to his upbringing in an environment where the idea of a good religious education was paramount.

Between the ages of 11 and 13 he attended the Herzliah High School in Montreal. It was the only Jewish day school in the city, set up in the 1930s as an alternative to the city's Catholic and Protestant school systems, so that Jewish children could learn about their own religious heritage.

Leonard Cohen came from a religiously committed home and would have been one of the High School's more advanced pupils when it came to religious education. He would almost certainly have known how to read Hebrew before he started at the school. Unlike most of his classmates.

The biggest challenge that Jewish children face when learning about their religion is getting to grips with the Hebrew language. All important Jewish texts, from the Hebrew Bible onwards, are written in Hebrew. It was the language in which the vast majority of prayers were recited in Montreal's synagogues. A year or two hence, at the age of 13, the boys would celebrate their bar mitzvah by reading a passage from a Torah scroll. Without the ability to read Hebrew they could neither do this nor, indeed, make much use of a Jewish prayer book.

But the Hebrew language has a different alphabet, and its vowels are written beneath the consonants. It bears no resemblance to English. Not only are most children daunted by it; they can't see any good reason why they should bother to learn it. For centuries Hebrew teachers have struggled to motivate their pupils. One medieval strategy was to write the alphabet on a slate and then smear honey over the top. The kids were allowed to lick the honey off each letter as they learned it.

Leonard Cohen's class would have learned together about the festivals, biblical history and some of the prayers and rituals of Judaism. They'd have been taught about the struggle to create a Jewish state, about the kibbutz pioneers in Palestine reclaiming the land from malarial swamp. They'd have sung the songs the kibbutzniks sang, but would probably have only heard sanitized accounts about the fighting in Palestine between the Jews and Arabs, and the hapless attempts of the forces of the British mandate to retain control. And they had heard about the Holocaust: the full extent of the destruction was not yet known, but gruesome reports of the slaughter were already emerging. There was no way that the horrors could be kept away from lively-minded schoolchildren.

As one of the few who could read Hebrew, Cohen would have been taken out of the main Jewish Studies class and put in a group to study the Torah more intensely. It would have been here that he had his first exposure to the sources that he would draw on many years later in his poems and music.

Typically children of his age in the 1940s began their Bible study with some of the better-known narratives: stories about Abraham, Isaac and Jacob, the birth of Moses, the Burning Bush and the Exodus from Egypt. They would read them in the original biblical Hebrew, slowly, translating each word as they went along. When they first started, if they got through a whole biblical sentence in one lesson their teachers said they were making good progress. Gradually, they would speed up, until they reached a certain fluency with the biblical text. Then they were introduced to Rashi's commentary.

Rashi is the Jewish biblical commentator *par excellence*. He is always referred to as Rashi, an acronym of his full name, Rabbi Shlomo Yitzhaki. He lived in Troyes, on the River Seine, in the early part of the twelfth century. He was a grape farmer by trade. The reason why this thousand-year-old French scholar is still regarded as the pre-eminent biblical commentator of all time is that he is so easy to understand. He was phenomenally economical with language. Rashi can say in three words what most of us need a couple of sentences to express. And it is not just that he is concise; his comments are always deeply rooted in the ancient Jewish tradition. Rashi is not read for his originality of thought. He is studied for his faithful, succinct explanations of the simple meaning of the Bible, for identifying and resolving biblical inconsistencies, ambiguities and conundrums with a mere flourish of his quill.

Bible with Rashi's commentary was probably the most advanced subject the 12-year-old Leonard Cohen studied at Herzliah High School. The pinnacle of Jewish learning, the study of the Talmud, was likely to have still been some years away.

Rashi frequently alludes to the folklore of the Talmud and Midrash. His commentary opened Leonard Cohen up to a whole new genre of Jewish literature, some of which he may have heard as nursery tales when a young child. He may have recalled the story of how Moses got his stammer. Pharaoh, so the legend goes, felt threatened by the sharp-witted infant his daughter had found lying in a basket among the bulrushes and adopted as her own. He decided to test the child by placing a lump of gold and a glowing coal in front of him. If Moses went for the coal instead of the gold, Pharaoh would know that the boy was just a dullard, of no threat to the royal throne. But if he chose to pick up the gold, he would have demonstrated his intelligence. Pharaoh would have no choice but to eliminate him.

Moses looked at the glowing coal and the nugget of gold; he didn't need to hesitate. As he reached to pick up the gold, an angel shot down from heaven and directed his hand towards the coal. The child picked it up and, as little children do, put it to his mouth. It saved his life but he singed his lip. From that time on Moses was, as he told God at the Burning Bush, 'slow of speech and slow of tongue'.[37]

The three years that Leonard Cohen spent at Herzliah High School gave him his first intensive exposure to the legends and stories that Jewish tradition superimposed on the biblical text. Many of these legends were constructed to appeal to and engage children, so that they would recall them as adults and teach them to their own offspring. Or, if they were particularly talented, they might even weave them into the stories they would write themselves. Or use them in their poetry and in their music.

BY THE RIVERS DARK
Ten New Songs (2001)

> **By the rivers dark,**
> **I wandered on.**
> **I lived my life**
> **In Babylon.**

Rabbi Yeremiya, a Talmudic scholar who lived in Israel in the fourth century, was scathing when he heard how one of his fellow rabbis in Babylon had answered a question. 'Foolish Babylonians,' he said. 'Because they live in a dark place they come up with dull answers.' Babylon, in Yeremiya's mind, was a dark place. Not because it was lacking in light, but because he thought it a place devoid of wisdom and common sense, full of people with dull minds.[38]

By the Rivers Dark is Cohen's adaptation, with a twist, of Psalm 137, 'By the Rivers of Babylon'. The rivers are dark in his version of the psalm because he too thought Babylon a dark place. Though not for the same reasons as Rabbi Yeremiya.

Cohen wasn't the first contemporary singer to adapt this psalm: it was popularized in the 1970s by the Jamaican reggae band The Melodians. It subsequently became an international hit when Boney M covered it. The reggae versions were fairly faithful transcriptions of the biblical text, quoting the first half of the psalm and adding a final line from Psalm 19. Cohen's adaptation, as we might expect, owed nothing to the earlier recordings and took the song in a completely different direction from that of the original psalm.

Psalm 137 is often cited as evidence that King David could not possibly have written the entire book of Psalms: it describes events that took place four centuries after he lived. It is a lament ostensibly sung by a group of Hebrew captives living in Babylon, yearning for their homeland and their old way of life. They had been taken into exile when the Babylonian armies of King Nebuchadnezzar conquered their land at the beginning of the sixth century BCE. Nebuchadnezzar destroyed Jerusalem and its Temple, carrying away its king, its leading citizens and many of its inhabitants. The Hebrew prophets had been warning for some time that this would happen. The forthcoming exile, they had said, would be a punishment for the nation's failure to worship the one true God as they had been commanded. The prophets didn't attach too much blame to Nebuchadnezzar; they regarded him as the unwitting instrument of God's wrath. Unlike the Egyptian Pharaoh who enslaved the Hebrews, Nebuchadnezzar is not particularly vilified in the Jewish tradition.

The biblical books of Kings and Chronicles record Nebuchadnezzar's invasion of the land and the war that led to Jerusalem's destruction. They do not pay very much attention to the suffering of the individuals caught up in the slaughter and the exile. That is left to Psalm 137. It tells of the captives sitting, weeping, beneath the willows that grew alongside Babylon's great watercourses: the rivers Euphrates and Tigris, and the network of canals that crossed between them. The captives were probably musicians, for the psalm recounts that they hung their harps in the trees when they their captors mocked them, demanding that they sing songs of their homeland. 'Sing for us a song of Zion,' the Babylonian captors gloated. 'How can we sing the Lord's song upon a foreign soil?' the captives replied.[39]

The captives grew bitter as their sense of loss sank in. They vowed never to forget Jerusalem, swearing that their memory of its destruction would always take precedence over any happiness that might come their way. Should they fail to remember Jerusalem, they adjured their right hands to lose their power, their tongues to cleave to the roofs of their mouths. They cursed Babylon, wishing for its inhabitants to suffer, in equal measure, everything that they themselves had endured. Finally, in what must be the most vicious and disturbing verse in the Bible, they wished happiness on anyone who violently slaughtered Babylonian babies.[40] The reggae version of *Rivers of Babylon* ends long before reaching this conclusion.

Cohen mentions Babylon several times in his poetry and music. But the Babylon he sings of is not the Babylon of history, the Babylon that was the dominant power in the Middle East in the sixth century BCE. That Babylon was a city – fabulous by all accounts, one of the wonders of the ancient world – with hanging gardens and ziggurats, high towers, stepped like stairways reaching to the skies. It was in Babylon, or Babel as it is known in the Bible, that the greatest engineers of the ancient world tried to build a tower stretching to heaven. The Tower of Babel.

The Babylonian empire was destroyed in 539 BCE, shortly after Nebuchadnezzar's reign, and the city gradually crumbled and disintegrated. But the name lived on, and people still referred to the region to the south of modern Baghdad as Babylon. Rabbi Yeremiya, who dismissed his Babylonian colleagues as foolish, lived a thousand years after the city's demise.

Cohen's interest in Babylon owes nothing to his Jewish upbringing. Even though it was a place to which the Jews were exiled, and was for many centuries the centre of Jewish learning and the heart of the diaspora, the idea of Babylon is not a Jewish trope. Cohen would never had heard anyone speak about Babylon in the synagogue. The Babylon of notoriety, the image that excited Leonard Cohen's attention, comes from the book of Revelation, the book with which the New Testament concludes. Written towards the end of the first or early in the second century CE, Revelation is a terrifying book, full of weird, apocalyptic imagery and bizarre symbols:

Babylon the great, mother of whores and of earth's abominations ... It has become a dwelling place of demons, a haunt of every foul spirit, a haunt of every foul bird, a haunt of every foul and hateful beast. For all the nations have drunk of the wine of the wrath of her fornication, and the kings of the earth have committed fornication with her and the merchants of the earth have been rich from the power of her luxury.[41]

Leonard Cohen's Babylon is a metaphor for materialism, sin and corruption. In his early song, *Last Year's Man*, recorded in 1970, Cohen sang of an erotic wedding ceremony in which Bethlehem had been the bridegroom and Babylon was an impassioned, seductive bride. Then in 1974, in *Is This What You Wanted?*, a bitter song about a decaying relationship, he sang 'You were the whore and the beast of Babylon'. Babylon to Cohen symbolizes the corruption of the world in which we live. It is a hedonistic city, a place of pleasure and sin. His ditty *Dance Me to the End of Love*, an astonishing amalgamation of sensual poetry and Holocaust imagery, contains the line 'Let me feel you moving, like they do in Babylon'.

In a 2001 interview he told the French magazine *L'Optimum*: 'Babylon is what I call "Boogie Street", this is where we are with no real possibility of escaping.'[42] 'Boogie Street', he told us in his song of the same name, is where he kept finding himself returning to after experiencing a spiritual insight, the place of traffic jams and normal life, a place whose purpose he didn't understand.

> **And I did forget**
> **My holy song.**

The captive Israelite that Cohen sings about in *By the Rivers Dark* has a different attitude from those in Psalm 137. In the psalm the captives are sitting by the river, weeping, yearning to return home. They have hidden their harps in the trees so that they cannot be forced to sing songs for their captors. But Cohen's captive is not so cowed. He is wandering by the rivers, soaking up the environment, trying to make the most of Babylonian life. He is assimilating into Babylonian culture, his desire to assimilate so strong that, unlike the psalm's captives, who refused to sing the Lord's song in this foreign land, he has put the holy song out of his mind altogether. Rather than a lament, this is the song of an exile who has been so absorbed into the alien culture in which he finds himself that he no longer remembers where he came from or who he used to be.

> **By the rivers dark**
> **Where I could not see**
> **Who was waiting there**
> **Who was hunting me.**

But, much as our Israelite exile believes that he is being absorbed into Babylonian life, he is not safe. His experience is that of the outsider, the refugee in an alien culture – in his case the age-old Jew driven from his land, trying to fit in wherever he finds himself. He doesn't know who is hunting him, but he knows that he is a prey, that someone, or something, is waiting for him.

Leonard Cohen, born one year after Hitler came to power, who lived safely in Canada while Europe was being ravaged, could nevertheless not avoid being touched by the Holocaust. Like all Jews of his generation, he had relatives killed in the Holocaust. His grandfather, who arrived in Canada before Hitler came to power, had been the head of a *yeshiva*, a rabbinical college, in Kovno, a Lithuanian town where the entire Jewish population was slaughtered.

In 1964 Leonard Cohen published a book of poems, *Flowers for Hitler*, about which he said:

> It's taking the mythology of the concentration camps and bringing it into the living room and saying this is what we do to each other. We outlawed genocide and concentration camps and gas and that, but if a man leaves his wife or they are cruel to each other, then that cruelty is going to find a manifestation ... the fact is that we all succumb to lustful thoughts to evil thoughts to thoughts of torture.[43]

He quoted from Primo Levi in the foreword: 'If from the inside of the Lager, a message could have seeped out to free men, it would have been this: Take care not to suffer in your own homes what is inflicted on us here.'

Cohen's captive in Babylon who tried so hard to integrate that he even forgot the holy song of his homeland, is perturbed to find that, like the cultured, assimilated Jews of pre-war Germany, he is still regarded as an outsider by the native population. He is a prey, a quarry to be chased down by invisible pursuers; he will suffer the fate of all who are different in sinful Babylon. He is hunted.

And he cut my lip
And he cut my heart
So I could not drink
From the rivers dark.

Nor does his alienation end there. He is even physically incapable of benefiting from his new society, from his life in Babylon. The captives in the psalm had sworn that if they forgot Jerusalem their right hands should wither and their tongues cleave to the roofs of their mouths.[44] This vow was sufficient to ensure they would never forget their homeland. Cohen's captive has not made such a vow. But the outcome is the same; he is wounded, mutilated. Not only has he forgotten Jerusalem and not only can he not sing the holy song of Zion, but he is also unable to drink from the dark rivers. He cannot take full advantage of the sinful, wanton life that Babylon offers.

In the psalm the body parts that the Israelite captives pledge as a surety against forgetting their homeland are the right hand and the tongue. Cohen has changed these to lip and heart. He is alluding to a couple of obscure biblical phrases that help to explain what has happened to his captive.

Both obscure phrases are connected with the idea of circumcision. Not a physical circumcision of the body but a spiritual circumcision, a liberation of the soul. At the Burning Bush, when God told Moses to return to Egypt, confront Pharaoh and liberate the Israelites, Moses argued that he could not possibly take on the task, for 'I am uncircumcised of lip'. This is usually taken to mean that he stammered, that he was not a fluent speaker, not a communicator. He could neither negotiate with Pharaoh nor lead the people to freedom. They wouldn't listen to him. Later, in the book of Deuteronomy, Moses, who through years of experience has now learned how to lead and communicate, tells the Israelites that in order to do God's will, they must 'circumcise the foreskins of your heart so that your necks will no longer be stiff'. To be circumcised of heart means to remove the spiritual defect of obstinacy, of being stiff-necked.

The cure for both these deficiencies, obstinacy and the inability to communicate, is, the Bible implies, to undergo a spiritual circumcision, to liberate one's soul through a metaphorical cutting away of the impediment.[45] Cohen's captive has had his defects removed; his heart and lip have been metaphorically cut.

Circumcised of heart and lip, he has been returned by his captors to the state that the Bible regards as ideal. He is no longer stiff-necked, and he can now express himself verbally. But now that he has been perfected spiritually, he is no longer capable of drinking from the dark, sinful waters.

> **Then he struck my heart**
> **with a deadly force**
> **and he said 'This heart**
> **It is not yours'.**
> **And he gave the wind**
> **My wedding ring.**

Cohen's metaphors are growing opaque. In the psalm the captives called upon God to avenge the brutality of the Babylonians. But Cohen's captive doesn't need to invoke God's assistance. For he begins to undergo a metamorphosis. He is told that his heart is not his, then his wedding ring is cast to the wind. His identity is about to change.

The heart, as far as the Bible is concerned, is the seat of the soul, the centre of our spiritual identity. Cohen's captive is being prepared to receive a new heart. At the same time his wedding ring is thrown to the wind. The wedding ring represents the kabbalistic notion of a mystical union with God. Having it thrown to the wind suggests that the captive is finally being torn from his Israelite identity, that the new heart he will receive will implant in him the true spirit of Babylon.

I live my life
In Babylon ...
Though I take my song
From a withered limb
Both song and tree
They sing for him.

Now his transformation is complete. Against all the odds he has managed to assimilate into Babylon, to become a member of Babylonian society and to enjoy all the hedonistic pleasures Babylon offers. Yet he has not offended against his God, his people or his homeland. He has done what the Bible demanded of him: his heart and lip are circumcised and his soul is liberated. Now he can sing his song. He is not like the other captives who hung their harps in the trees and vowed that their hands should wither if they sang. His experience may have wounded him, but he can oblige the captor who demanded a song of Zion. Drawing his song down from the tree, where the captives hung their harps, he can both sing it and live the life he wants to live, in Babylon.

> **Be the truth unsaid,**
> **and the blessing gone,**
> **if I forget my Babylon.**

It is possible, Cohen is telling us, to become part of a new culture yet still to retain one's ethnic and cultural identity. We don't need to cling to the old and reject the new, like the captives who hung their harps in the trees and refused to accept the reality of their changed situation. Nor do we need to reject our past completely by becoming identical to those we now live among. They will only rebuff us if we try.

When we find ourselves straddling two cultures, unable to work out where we fit in, the solution lies somewhere between the two. 'If I forget thee Jerusalem …' wept the captives in Psalm 137. Not so, we hear Leonard Cohen say. We can benefit from both Zion and Babylon. As he later explained:

> A lot of the songs on the album are about that, about the reconciliation between these two ways of life, because ultimately, it may very well be that this holy city of Jerusalem sits right in the middle of the kingdom of sins, and that we are prisoners of these two kingdoms which are one forever.[46]

BORN IN CHAINS
Popular Problems (2014)

I was born in chains
But I was taken out of Egypt,
I was bound to a burden,
But the burden it was raised.

Leonard Cohen once said that *Born in Chains* took him longer to write than any other song. 'That's been kicking around for 40 years,' he told *Rolling Stone* magazine. 'I've rewritten the lyric many times to accommodate the changes in my theological position, which is very insecure.'[47] Originally called *Taken out of Egypt*, the song was finally performed during his 2010 tour, with Cohen changing the lyrics frequently as the tour progressed. He recorded the song on the 2014 album *Popular Problems*.

Popular Problems was received with greater enthusiasm than any other Leonard Cohen album. He was 80 years old when it was released. It topped the charts across the world, although it peaked at only number 15 in the United States. Cohen's popularity in the USA never reached the levels it did in Europe or Canada.

Born in Chains is based on the biblical story of the exodus of the Israelites from Egypt. But in Cohen's version it is the story of an individual, not the Israelite nation. He had been born as a slave, in chains; when he was liberated from Egypt the burden that had weighed him down was raised. So far the song could be about anyone who has been liberated from physical or psychological oppression. But then Cohen sings:

Lord I can no longer, keep this secret.
Blessed is the Name, the Name be praised.

And we find ourselves being challenged by a song that takes us to the heart of mystical theology, a song that is not at all easy to understand, let alone to explain.

We have come across the Name before and we will come across it again. Leonard Cohen sang about it in *Hallelujah*, he will sing about it in several of the songs this book explores. It is the name of God, the unknowable, unutterable, Name, the correct pronunciation of which is a closely guarded secret. It was last publicly pronounced, according to tradition, by the High Priest in the Jerusalem Temple, before the sanctuary was destroyed by the Romans in the year 70 CE. As his surname indicates, Leonard Cohen was descended from the temple priests. But the secret that he cannot keep is not the secret pronunciation of the Name.

We will have to wait until later in the song to find out what the secret is that Cohen cannot keep. But his exclamation 'Blessed is the name' is a common idiom in modern Hebrew, equivalent to something like 'Thank God' in English. It is also the opening of a liturgical response: 'Blessed be the name of his glorious kingdom.' But Cohen is not ready to tell us what his secret is, or why he is blessing the Name.

I fled to the edge,
Of the Mighty Sea of Sorrow…
But the waters parted,
And my soul crossed over.

When the liberated Israelites fled from Egypt, with Pharaoh's armies hotly pursuing them, they found themselves driven up against the impenetrable barrier of the Red Sea. With Pharaoh to their rear and the sea in front, there was nowhere for them to go. They cried out to God and complained to Moses. They told him that they knew they should never have left Egypt, that they were better off as slaves. In the earliest example of the art of Jewish grumbling they ask whether there weren't enough graves in Egypt, so that they had to be brought into the wilderness to die.

Moses got no sympathy from God either. 'Why are you crying to me?' he demanded of Moses. 'Tell the Children of Israel to keep going. Lift up your staff and stretch out your arm.' Moses did so, and miraculously the waters parted. The Israelites passed through the sea on dry land. When the Egyptians tried to follow, the waters returned and engulfed them.[48]

Cohen called the Red Sea the '**Sea of Sorrow**'. He is alluding to a Talmudic legend in which the angels were rebuked when God heard them rejoicing over the destruction of the Egyptian army: 'My creations are drowning and you want to sing a song!'[49]

The biblical story of the crossing of the Red Sea is the first part in a two-part drama. Crossing the sea, escaping the Egyptians, freed the Israelites from slavery. As a nation they were physically liberated. But physical liberty is not enough, as Cohen is explaining in this song. True liberty is freedom of the soul as well as the body. In the Bible, the Israelites, Cohen's soul among them, got their spiritual freedom a few weeks after crossing the Red Sea, when they reached Mount Sinai. Moses went up the mountain and God gave him the Ten Commandments, engraved on two tablets of stone.

In Hebrew, the word meaning 'engraved' is very similar to the word for 'freedom'. The Talmud, in one of its characteristic puns, declares: 'Do not read it as "engraved on the tablets", read it as "freedom on the tablets".'[50] The giving of the Ten Commandments on Mount Sinai was the moment when the Israelites became spiritually liberated; it complemented and completed their physical liberation at the Red Sea.

Blessed is the Name
The Name be blessed,
Written on my heart
In burning Letters
That's all I know
I cannot read the rest.

God proclaimed the Ten Commandment to Moses in an earthquake of unimaginable intensity. The heavenly horn was blown, the mountain trembled, thunder raged and lightning flashed. Midrashic legend says that when God spoke, the letters of each word appeared in heaven, written in black fire upon white fire. They flew over the camp of the Israelites, spinning and whirling before alighting on the tablets of stone. The Israelites, standing at the foot of the mountain hearing the tremendous power of God's voice, witnessing the terrifying spectacle of the blazing letters thrashing through the air, ran away. 'You speak with us,' they told Moses, 'and we will listen, but don't let God speak to us, lest we die.'[51]

Cohen's soul, which had crossed the Red Sea, shared in this experience. But he cannot read the words on the tablets. As for the other Israelites, it is all too much for him. The fiery letters have burned the Name upon his heart, but he cannot decipher anything else. His heart was branded by the fire of the letters, until he could bear no more. He is reliving the experience of Sinai, the event at which every Jew is obliged to imagine they witnessed.[52]

> **I was idle with my soul …**
> **My life remained the same**
> **Then you showed me**
> **Where you had been wounded**
> **In every atom**
> **Broken is the Name.**

The giving of the Ten Commandments should have been a moment of spiritual transformation for Cohen, bestowed against the backdrop of a stirring, awe-inspiring mythology.

But Cohen is only human – one who sees himself as flawed, living in a fractured world. He is idle, he believes; his soul has failed to live up to the moment. And the failure is not just his to bear alone. His inadequacies have cosmic repercussions.

When Leonard Cohen sings '**Broken is the Name**', he is singing of the only thing we can know about God: his Name. God is hidden and unreachable; only his Name is heard in the world. But the Name, Cohen says, is broken.

'Broken' is a word that characterizes Leonard Cohen's view of the world. In the foreword to Cohen's posthumously published book *The Flame*, his son Adam notes that certain words crop up time and time again in Cohen's work. 'Broken' is one of them; others include 'frozen', 'naked', 'flame' and 'fire'.

A fundamental concept in Kabbalah is that while the world remains in its present chaotic state God's Name is sundered from his essence – '**wounded in every atom**', as Cohen puts it. Humanity's task is to unite God's essence with his Name, to transform the cosmos and our human perception so that God can be perceived in all his immanence. As the prophet Zechariah puts it: 'In that day, God will be One and his name will be One.'[53] But until then, as Cohen sings, '**Broken is the Name**'.

In the Grip
Of sensual illusion
A sweet unknowing
Unified the Name.

While the Name is broken, salvation is remote. But one of the joys of being human is that we do not need to live in the spiritual world. The world we inhabit may be a world of illusion, as Cohen knew from his immersion in Zen, but it is the illusory world from which we derive our immediate pleasures. The Name can be unified through '**sensual illusion**'. And so Cohen turns to the holiest of all acts, where creation and passion intersect. As he once said: 'If you leave God out of sex, it becomes pornographic; if you leave sex out of God, it becomes self-righteous.'[54]

And through the physical act of love Cohen finds a remedy. For himself and for the broken Name. Ultimately it all comes down to love.

We are left with the question of the secret Cohen could not keep. What had he learned that was too powerful for him, that he could not express, that led him to exclaim, '**Blessed is the Name**'?

The biblical character who wants to disclose a secret but finds himself unable to do so is the Patriarch Jacob, who led the Israelites into their Egyptian exile, the exile from which Cohen's soul was liberated. On his deathbed in Egypt Jacob summoned his sons: 'Gather together and I will tell you what will happen to you at the End of Days,' he says. He wants to reveal the forbidden secrets of the end of time to them, to disclose the unknowable future. But he does not. Instead he starts to give them his dying blessing. A midrashic legend explains that, as soon as he made up his mind to reveal forbidden matters, the prophetic spirit departed from him.

Jacob didn't understand why he had been denied the spirit of prophecy. Was there something wrong with his sons that made them unworthy of knowing what he knew? He asked them if they were wholehearted in their faith in God. When they reassured him he exclaimed: 'Blessed be the Name ...'[55]

Cohen's secret was not Jacob's; he didn't have knowledge of what will happen at the end of time. The secret he could no longer keep was resolved for him 'in the grip of sensual illusion'. It was the realization that intimacy is divine, that intimacy leads to revelation. The Name may be unified through the physical act of lovemaking. And the cry that he exclaimed as he experienced his sensual illusion, at the climax of his revelation, was the cry of his biblical ancestor Jacob. 'Blessed be the Name.' There is no blasphemy in intimacy.

SAMSON IN NEW ORLEANS
Popular Problems (2014)

> **You said that you were with me,**
> **You said you were my friend,**
> **Did you really love the city,**
> **Or did you just pretend?...**

The story of Samson in the biblical book of Judges is one of betrayal, revenge and a considerable amount of stupidity. Cohen uses the story to deliver a damning condemnation of the authorities in New Orleans in the years leading up to Hurricane Katrina. It is one of only a few instances of Leonard Cohen using his music to address a topical political issue.

Samson was the strongman of ancient Israel. Before he was born, an angel had told his mother that as long as his hair was never cut or shaved, and provided he never drank wine or anything else made from grapes, he would be Israel's saviour, delivering them from the Philistine enemy. The angel neglected to tell his mother to keep him away from Philistine women. That was a mistake, it turned out that Philistine women were his one real weakness. He couldn't stop himself from falling in love with them.

When he was still young, Samson married a Philistine woman. But the marriage ended in disaster after she told her countrymen the answer to a riddle that he had set them as a wager. Samson felt betrayed. He had only told her the answer because she cajoled him, and she had only cajoled him because the Philistines had put her under extreme pressure to find out the answer.

Samson was furious when he realized what had happened. He took his revenge on the Philistines, they retaliated, he responded and matters escalated until his wife and her father were dead and Samson was in a murderous rage. He grabbed the jawbone of an ass and charged into the Philistine army, slaying a thousand men. But he didn't learn his lesson.

Twenty years later he fell in love with another Philistine woman. Her name was Delilah. The Philistines were well and truly fed up with Samson by now. They had tried and failed so often to kill him, and had suffered at his hands in revenge every time. They bribed Delilah to find out the secret of his tremendous strength, each Philistine lord promising her eleven hundred pieces of silver. Torn between the bribe, her loyalty to her people and her feelings for Samson, she begged him: 'Tell me in what is your great strength and with what might you be bound, to afflict you.'[56] Samson, sensing a trap, gave her a false answer. 'Bind me with seven damp cords which have never dried and I will become weak, I will be like any man.' Next morning, when he awoke, he found himself bound with seven damp cords, surrounded by Philistines. He snapped the cords off him as if they were tinder and chased the Philistines away. But he still didn't learn his lesson.

Twice more Delilah asked him to tell her the secret of his strength; twice more he gave her a false answer, and each time he awoke to find himself surrounded by Philistines, bound with the materials he had told her would weaken him. We might think that Samson would have wised up by now. But he hadn't.

Delilah meanwhile was distraught. She could see the reward money slipping away. 'You don't love me,' she said to Samson. 'How can you say you love me when your heart is not with me? You have deceived me three times and you have not told me the real secret of your strength.' Conflicted and gullible, Samson gave in and told her that his strength lay in his unshorn locks. Next morning, when he awoke, his hair had been shorn, the Philistines had bound him fast and this time he was unable to free himself.[57]

Samson lost his strength, the Philistines put his eyes out and he spent the rest of his life in gaol, blind. But he got his vengeance. To celebrate his capture, the Philistines gathered to hold a great festival in their temple. They brought Samson up from the dungeon to mock him, tying him to the pillars that supported the roof of the temple. Samson prayed that God would grant him strength one final time so that he could take his ultimate revenge. His prayer was answered; he strained and tugged at the pillars, until they came crashing down. The roof collapsed, crushing everyone inside, himself included. Betrayed by Delilah, Samson had his final victory over the Philistines.

You said how could this happen,
You said how can this be ...

There's other ways to answer …
Me, I'm blind with death and anger.

Samson in New Orleans tells the story of a city betrayed, of someone unable to make sense of what has happened, of a catastrophe beyond imagination. It was a response to Hurricane Katrina, which devastated New Orleans in August 2005, killing over a thousand people in the city and making tens of thousands more homeless. Although it was a natural catastrophe, many people claimed that the extent of the damage and the majority of the deaths were the result of an inadequate flood protection system, failed leadership and a delayed government response.

In Cohen's lyrics we are to imagine Samson in New Orleans. Samson, who knows about betrayal, about revenge, about the destruction of buildings, is accusing the authorities of deceiving the city. Did they really love it, he asks, or was it just a pretence? Did they really not understand how it could happen, how neglect can have such devastating consequences? Samson is enraged. He describes the suffering survivors, for whom relief was frequently tardy and inadequate, as a dishonoured remnant stranded on bridges of misery. A response is demanded.

So gather up the killers
Get everyone in town
Stand me by those pillars
Let me take this temple down.

Samson, enraged by the city's inadequate preparations and leadership wants to respond as he did with the Philistines. His solution may appear extreme – he goes on to sing that he knows there are other ways to deal with the problem – but he is **blind with death and anger**.

Samson in New Orleans appears on the *Popular Problems* album, issued in 2014, nine years after the hurricane. This was not a delayed reaction on Cohen's part. Songs could take him years to write; he would famously write and discard verses continually until he was happy with what he had. We know that he was deeply touched by the New Orleans disaster; on his previous album, *Old Ideas*, his song *Banjo* describes him watching a broken instrument that is bobbing on a dark expanse of water. He didn't know how the banjo had got there; perhaps it fell from someone's shoulder, or had been washed up from a grave. 'After Katrina … I saw that culture dismantled, and I think that the image of a broken banjo floating in the dark came out of that deep discomfort that had been imposed on all our psyches.'[58]

> **There's a woman in the window**
> **And a bed in Tinsel Town**
> **I'll write you when it's over**
> **Let me take this temple down.**

For Cohen, Samson's story prefigures the events in New Orleans. But those who carry prime responsibility for the extent of the suffering heaped on the city will not be punished as he punished the Philistines. The temple, he knows, will not be brought down upon the heads of the city's authorities. Ultimately he is impotent in his rage. All he can do is to return, seething, to his daily life, and look forward to a time, which may never come, when he will be able to take revenge on those who deserve it.

3

IDEAS FROM THE BIBLE

Long before he got into the music business, Leonard Cohen had acquired a reputation as a poet and novelist. His first real musical break came when he sent arrangements of two of his poems, *Suzanne* and *Dress Rehearsal Rag*, to the folk singer Judy Collins. She recorded them on her album *In My Life*. The LP stayed in the USA charts for 34 weeks and propelled Cohen from up-and-coming poet to nascent songwriter.

Cohen spoke about his hopes for a musical career in an interview for a student newspaper. He told the interviewer, the future biographer Sandra Djwa, that he was in a 'capsule ... [which] is that of cantor – a priest of a catacomb religion that is underground, just beginning, and I am one of the many singers, one of the many, many priests, not by any means a high priest, but one of the creators of the liturgy that will create the church.'[1]

Cohen believed his new underground religion would serve the world in a way in which that the established faiths were no longer able. It was an idealistic ambition, somewhat naïve, but no more so than many ideas in 1967, a time when we all thought we could change the world. Although there is no indication that Cohen persisted with this aspiration (he is not on record as mentioning it again), it gives us an insight into his attitude to religion and the role of Judaism and Christianity in his life.

Despite his emotional connection to his native faith and the synagogue rituals of his childhood, much of the appeal of both Judaism and Christianity for Cohen lay in the literature of the Bible. But not necessarily in the way its messages had been interpreted in practice. The Bible spoke to him personally – he had no need of priests or rabbis to tell him what it meant. And sometimes it refuted the very things the priests and rabbis expected him to believe. Particularly when it came to the injustice in the world. 'Tell me again,' he challenged them in *Amen*, 'When the victims are singing, And Laws of Remorse are restored.' Or, in *That Don't Make It Junk*, railing against the seemingly impossible virtuous life the Bible demanded of him:

> You raise me up in grace,
> Then you put me in a place,
> Where I must fall.

Reading the Bible was for Leonard Cohen not simply a question of querying its assurances and prophecies. He obliged himself to understand and to come to terms with scripture, to allow himself to be challenged by it, to read beneath the surface and make sense of what it said to him. In *Democracy*, where he sings of how the USA will be transformed by the changing political tide, he tells us that he doesn't pretend to understand the Sermon on the Mount at all. But that doesn't stop him from recognizing the Sermon's staggering nature, from acknowledging that its oratory and message are transformational, that he has more to do to if he is to comprehend it. Democracy, he says, is unstoppable; it will emanate from everything and everyone. But of all its wellsprings, of all the many joys and tragedies, revolutions and disappointments that he lists, which, he believes will lead to the transfiguration of America, it is only the Sermon of the Mount that causes him to pause, to interrupt the catalogue of events he is reciting and confess that it holds a challenge to his understanding.

Cohen seems to have read the Bible holistically, as a homogeneous work of literature, in which each Testament and book carried equal authority, without prioritizing one part over another. As a result he treated each faith, Judaism and Christianity, equally, finding value in each, yet able to compare and contrast them. Even though he accused the established faiths of failing to make good on their promises, they dominated his thinking to a far greater extent than any 1960s aspirations he may have had of being the priest of a new underground faith.

But we do see an evolution in his attitudes as he grew older. Many young Jews become disillusioned with their faith, and, as the speech at the Montreal Jewish Public Library showed, Leonard Cohen was no exception. This might explain why he displays a greater affinity in his earlier music for the religion of the New Testament than of the Old. However, as the years went by, we see a tension develop, his reading of the Bible drawing him closer to an understanding of Judaism that resonated more closely with his core values and beliefs, until a time came when he was able to put the two faiths, Christianity and Judaism, into perspective and gain a better idea of where he stood with each of them. There is, as we shall see, a world of difference between the innocence of *Suzanne* and the disillusionment of *It Seemed the Better Way*.

SUZANNE
Songs of Leonard Cohen (1967)

And Jesus was a sailor
When he walked upon the water
And he spent a long time watching
From his lonely wooden tower.

Cohen came late to the record business. It was 1967 when he made his first album, *Songs of Leonard Cohen*, on which *Suzanne* is the opening track. The song had already been recorded by the folk singer Judy Collins. It wasn't going easily for him: agents would turn him down, thinking he was too old, that he dressed too soberly. Leonard Cohen just didn't fit into the hip 1960s music scene. Eventually he was introduced to Mary Martin, one of the few women in the music business at the time, who had worked her way up from a hostess job to being the head of her own artist management company. 'She was instrumental in bringing The Band and Dylan together,' Cohen told a BBC interviewer. 'She managed Van Morrison for a period. She was a very enterprising and very sensitive woman ... and very supportive.'

When Mary Martin introduced Cohen to Judy Collins, she was captivated by his poetry. She recorded *Suzanne* and *Dress Rehearsal Rag* on her new album. She and Cohen became friends but never lovers, and she helped him to become established in the Greenwich Village folk scene. Judy was the first person to encourage him to perform on stage, asking him to join her in a benefit concert in New York. The line-up included Tom Paxton and Pete Seeger.

Cohen was reluctant; he hesitated before coming on stage. When he did finally walk on, he couldn't tune his guitar and had to borrow Judy's. Then his voice gave up. He said, 'I can't do this', and left again. Had Judy Collins not persisted, encouraging him to return later in the concert, he might never had become a professional musician at all. He was approaching his 33rd birthday, in an era when most popular musicians had begun their careers in their teens or early twenties.

Cohen had already made something of a name for himself as a poet in his home city of Montreal, as a member of the city's small but vibrant literary scene. He won his first poetry prize in 1954. He published his first collection of poetry, *Let Us Compare Mythologies*, in 1956. Over the next couple of years he studied in New York, gave poetry readings in Montreal, spent a summer as a counsellor at a camp for Jewish children and, when he ran out of money, took a job in his family's clothing firm. In 1959 he received a grant of $2,000 from the Canada Council to write a novel set in the historic capital cities of Europe. He applied for a passport and flew to London.

One month before the 1960s started, Cohen arrived in what would eventually be known as 'Swinging London'. With his friend Nancy Bacal, another Jew from Montreal, whose father had been his paediatrician, Cohen went to the clubs and explored the late-night hangouts. The Twist was becoming the latest dance craze, and Cohen began to dance. He wrote to his older sister Esther that he really enjoyed it. 'I sometimes even forget that I belong to an inferior race ... The Twist is the greatest ritual since circumcision ... Myself, I prefer the Twist.'[3]

Despite the vibrancy of its music and cultural scene, Cohen did not find life in London easy. He lived in a boarding house in Hampstead run by Stella Pullman, a landlady who was used to having young artists staying with her. She did her best to make sure her tenants stuck to their work and didn't get distracted by the appeal of city life. When Cohen told her he was writing a novel, she informed him that his duty was to write three pages every day, and to take up the coal into the house from the cellar. She would check his work each day, and if he hadn't taken up the coal and written his three pages he would not be allowed to stay there.

> It was under her fierce and compassionate surveillance that I wrote my first novel, *The Favourite Game*, at the corner of Gayton Road and Hampstead High Street, so I do have some deep feelings about those moments I spent there.[4]

Although the boarding house he lived in was in Hampstead, one of the higher and greener parts of London, the city in those days was frequently shrouded in smog. He found it dark and depressing. An acquaintance, Jacob Rothschild, told him that his mother lived on an island in Greece that had, he said, a flourishing artists' colony. The island, just to the south east of the Peloponnese, was called Hydra. Rothschild suggested that Cohen pay the island a visit. Desperate for some warmth and sunshine, Cohen promptly boarded a plane. He spent a few days in Jerusalem, which was not quite on the way, then flew to Athens and finally took a ferry to the island. Hydra, it turned out, would be the place to which he would continually return for much of his life. A few months later, when his grandmother died, leaving him $1,500, he spent it all on a house on the island.

Life in Hydra was cheap and idyllic, but it didn't pay the bills. 'It was a very good way of living … but I couldn't pay my grocery bill, so I would come back to Canada, get various jobs, get that money together plus the boat fare, come back to Greece and live for as long as that money lasted.'[5]

It was on one of those trips back to Canada in the early 1960s that Cohen met Suzanne Verdal, a young Montreal dancer. She became something of a muse for him. He wrote two poems about her, publishing them both in his 1966 anthology *Parasites of Heaven*. He transformed one of the poems into his song *Suzanne*. The other, *Suzanne Wears a Leather Coat*, praises her striking beauty, describing how the traffic comes to a halt and people fall out of their cars as she walks by.

When they first met, Suzanne was living with one of Cohen's friends. That relationship soon broke up, but she and Cohen never became lovers. 'She would serve me Constant Comment tea which has little bits of oranges in it. And the boats were going by, and I touched her perfect body with my mind, because there was no other opportunity. There was no other way that you could touch her perfect body under those circumstances.'⁶

Cohen would visit her in her apartment in one of the old harbour buildings by the St Lawrence River, Montreal's main artery, where boats to and from the Atlantic would dock before the harbour was rebuilt in the 1950s. They would walk together by the dock, their walk taking them past the chapel of Notre-Dame-de-Bon-Secours, an iconic waterfront church, the oldest in Montreal. If Suzanne was the inspiration for the song that bears her name, Notre-Dame-de-Bon-Secours runs it a close second. The church's architecture features prominently in his lyrics.

On top of the church is a statue of the Virgin Mary. She stands, arms outstretched over the water, blessing the seafarers in the harbour. Known as Our Lady of the Harbour, the sun pours down upon her like honey, or so Cohen tells us in his song. Jesus, he says, keeps a perpetual vigil in the wooden observation tower that visitors to the church still climb. When they do, they find the lyrics to *Suzanne* written on its walls.

Notre-Dame-de-Bon-Secours is known as the Sailors' Church. Model boats hang from its ceiling. Seafarers prayed there before setting off on their voyages. Their prayers inspired the verse in *Suzanne* that begins 'and Jesus was a sailor when he walked upon the water'. Sandwiched between two verses about Suzanne, we get the impression that his affection for Jesus was secondary only to his tenderness for her. It is a love of Suzanne that he knows Jesus shares: in the first verse Cohen sings of touching her perfect body with his mind; in the second verse it is Jesus' mind that touches her perfect body.

> It was as though she handed me the seed for the song ... So Suzanne becomes an incarnation of that church for sailors, Notre-Dame-de-Bon-Secours or Our Lady of Consolation – that's her church. Suzanne becomes of course Our Lady of the Harbour, or she manifests as Our Lady of the Harbour ... Notre-Dame-de-Bon-Secours faces the river; the sailors are blessed from that church. So the next verse moves very easily to the idea that Jesus was a sailor.[7]

Jesus became a sailor when he climbed into a boat with his disciples, after famously walking on the waters of the Sea of Galilee. Now, in Cohen's song he is watching from the church's wooden tower until he is certain that he can only be seen by those drowning in the sea, those who have no boats, who are not sailors. The sea, he says, will free them.

> **And when he knew for certain**
> **Only drowning men could see him**
> **He said 'All men will be sailors then**
> **Until the sea shall free them.'**

Cohen may be alluding to baptism in the sea as a way of obtaining salvation. But there is an obscure legend, occurring in the little known apocryphal book *The History of Mar Matthew and Mar Andrew*, a Syriac text written some time after the third century, although the version that has survived is probably much later. The text tells the story of Andrew the apostle, a fisherman on the Sea of Galilee. He was sent on a mission to rescue his fellow apostle Matthew, who has been captured and imprisoned in a city of cannibals. In order to travel to the city Andrew goes down to the harbour, where he sees a boat containing three men. Unknown to him, two of the men are angels; the third, the steersman, is Jesus.

Arriving in the city, Andrew manages to free not only Matthew but also all the other prisoners locked up with him. Miraculously, he wreaks vengeance on the cannibals, until he is himself captured, tortured and thrown into prison. With Jesus' help Andrew creates a flood, submerging the city in water. Only then, as the inhabitants are drowning, do they realize the error of their ways. Andrew teaches them about Jesus, baptizes them and builds a church in the city. Freed by the water, the drowning men now recognize that their salvation has come through Jesus.[8] Might Leonard Cohen have come across this legend as he thought about the nautical church of Notre-Dame-de-Bon-Secours?

Christianity holds a spiritual attraction for Cohen that is qualitatively different from his commitment to Judaism. The songs and poems that he bases on Jewish ideas tend to be philosophical, mystical or defiant, whereas his works inspired by Christianity preach a simpler message, of love and purity of spirit. Unlike many religious people, particularly those who actively practise their faith, Cohen did not feel threatened by other systems of thought, nor did he seek to exclude them from his frame of reference. He had an almost unique ability to draw on the best of every belief system he encountered, and, as far as one can tell from his lyrics, he saw no conflict between any of them. They were all part of a greater, unified whole, a unity he devoted his life to seeking.

When he played *Suzanne*, Cohen would say how good he felt about the song because people loved it, and the rights to it were stolen from him. Cohen always said that this was actually fortunate: 'It would be wrong to write this song and get rich from it too.'[9]

LAST YEAR'S MAN
Songs of Love and Hate (1971)

Last Year's Man is a dark and despairing song. The lyrics dramatically capture Cohen's mood in the depths of a depression, when he found himself unable to write, draw or compose. As the song opens it is raining; he is holding a crayon but not drawing; his Jew's harp lies idle on the table and the blueprint of his latest work is scuffed and dog-eared. The skylight above him is cracked, giving it the appearance of a broken drumskin.

Then Joan of Arc makes an appearance. She is in the dark, playing with her soldiers; whether she is playing with them sexually or as a child might with her toys is not explained. Cohen cannot stay with her. He thanks her for treating him so well but, even though he is wearing a uniform, he tells he was not destined to fight. In the depths of his depression, Cohen cannot even find solace in Joan of Arc, his tragic, seductive, warrior muse.

Songs of Love and Hate, recorded in 1971, was Cohen's third album. If any of his albums justified the epithet 'music to commit suicide by', this was the one. His marriage to Suzanne wasn't working, and he was heavily into drugs. He had just come back from his first European tour, one he had never really wanted to go on, a tour that had been emotionally and physically draining.

It was the tour in which he got himself into a confrontation with the audience in Hamburg, shouting 'Sieg Heil' and goose-stepping on stage. But he'd also worked a miracle, at the Isle of Wight, where a fractious and rowdy crowd of half a million supposedly peace-loving hippies were well on the way to orchestrating a riot. Trampling the barriers and gates, they'd piled into a field that was intended to hold an audience of no more than 150,000. The organizers of the commercial festival had no choice but to turn it into a free event. The performers found themselves besieged. Kris Kristofferson had bottles thrown at him and was booed off stage. The Doors insisted on playing in the dark so the audience couldn't aim projectiles at them. Jimi Hendrix's set was cut short after one of the crowd set fire to the stage.

Then it was Cohen's turn. It was two in the morning. The crowd were seething. He was bombed on Mandrax, just as he had been in Hamburg. Cohen spoke to them, slowly, hypnotically; he'd learned a little of how to use hypnosis when he was younger. He asked them all to light a match, 'So we could locate one another. And could I ask you, each person, to light a match so that I could see where you all are? Could each of you light a match so that you will sparkle like fireflies, each at your different heights? I would love to see those matches flare.' Slowly they did, a few at first, then gradually more, holding the lights aloft. He started to tell them a story. They listened. He played *Suzanne*, read some poetry and played some more. He was on stage for nearly two hours. He built a rapport with the audience and calmed the crowd.[10]

The tour had been eventful and emotionally exhausting. And he had no time to get over it. When he got home, he was reminded that under his contract with his record company he now had to make a third album. It was the last straw. As he began recording, everything inside him started to fall apart. He lost his will; he was devoid of motivation. He began to hate the sound of his own voice, starting to believe the negative things people said about his music. He told a journalist: 'Sometimes I feel that my life is a sell-out and that I am the greatest comedian of my generation.'[11]

It was a difficult time for Cohen altogether. But *Last Year's Man* was more than just a chronicle of his mood at that particular moment. His depressions had been coming and going for years.

> **I came upon a wedding that old families had contrived;**
> **Bethlehem the bridegroom,**
> **Babylon the bride ...**
> **And when we fell together all our flesh was like a veil,**
> **That I had to draw aside to see the serpent eat its tail.**

In the third verse, after describing the state of his surroundings and his vision of Joan of Arc, Cohen finds himself at an erotic wedding, the marriage of Babylon and Bethlehem. Babylon, Cohen tells us, was naked, standing, trembling for him. Bethlehem was reticent, as shy as an inexperienced participant in an orgy. The three of them – Cohen, Bethlehem and Babylon – fell together, veiling something beneath their flesh. As he drew aside, Cohen saw that they were cloaking a serpent which was eating its tail. It's not an easy verse.

The image of Babylon as a bride is based on an interpretation of the book of Revelation. As we have seen, Cohen was particularly fascinated by Revelation, frequently using it as a source for several of his metaphors about corruption, wantonness and decay.

In a startling display of ancient misogyny, the author of Revelation portrayed Babylon as a woman sitting on a blasphemous, scarlet beast with seven heads and ten horns:

> And the woman was arrayed in purple and scarlet colour, and decked with gold and precious stones and pearls, having a golden cup in her hand full of abominations and filthiness of her fornication. And upon her forehead was a name written, 'Mystery, Babylon the Great, the Mother of Harlots and Abominations of the Earth'. And I saw the woman drunken with the blood of the saints, and with the blood of the martyrs of Jesus.[12]

This woman became known in Christian tradition as the Bride of Antichrist. She was the bride at the wedding Cohen came upon. But if she was the Bride of Antichrist, then what of her groom, Bethlehem? It seems that in Cohen's eyes that Bethlehem, the birthplace of both Jesus and his ancestor King David, must be the Antichrist himself.

Perhaps this isn't so strange when we consider that *Last Year's Man* is a song about someone in the depths of depression, when everything around him is bathed in the gloom of melancholy. When the Messianism of Bethlehem holds no promise and even the lasciviousness of Babylon fails to seduce. It explains why he sees 'the serpent eat its tail'. Even the serpent, the biblical symbol of temptation, is impotent in the face of extreme depression; it is reduced to consuming itself. There is no desire, no incentive and no drive. Nothing can penetrate the despondency Cohen feels.

> Some women wait for Jesus, and some women
>   wait for Cain ...
> And I take the one who finds me back to where it
>   all began
> When Jesus was the honeymoon
> And Cain was just the man ...
> The wilderness is gathering
> All its children back again.

But all is not doom and gloom. In the final verses of the song the depression lifts somewhat. Cohen perceives that the world is not monochromatic; not everything is based in the fog of his despair. Some women are drawn to the saviour, to Jesus, others to his opposite, the murderous Cain. These polarities imply that there is potential for change, for things to transition between extremes. Action is possible; he does not need to be subsumed in depression eternally. He can start again, go back to the time when everything began. When movement was possible, when Jesus held out a promise and Cain was innocent. Then the wilderness will summon back the Children of Israel, history will rewind and we will have the chance of a new beginning.

And now he returns to his opening verse. But not quite. An hour has passed, the rain is continuing to fall and he remains motionless; his hand has not moved. But there is a new couplet in the verse.

> **But everything will happen if he only gives the word**
> **The lovers will rise up**
> **And the mountains touch the ground.**

All he needs to do now, Cohen recognizes, is to give the word and things will begin to happen again. Until then the skylight will remain cracked and it will continue to rain.

The scriptural references in *Last Year's Man* illustrate the holistic way in which Leonard Cohen read the Bible and the unusual connections that he could draw between disparate parts of the text. Nowhere in the Bible are Babylon and Bethlehem directly contrasted with each other; nor are Jesus and Cain. In Revelation, Babylon is contrasted with Jerusalem, while in Genesis, Cain is paired with Abel. But Cohen was not concerned with traditional polarities; his connections were thematic: Bethlehem and Babylon are linked by the polarities of Christ and Antichrist, Jesus and Cain by the poles of good and evil.

Cohen liked *Last Year's Man*. But, as with so much of his work, he would not play or publish it until he was certain he'd got it right. In the album notes to his compilation *Best of Leonard Cohen* he wrote:

I don't know why but I like this song. I used to play it on a Mexican 12 string until I destroyed the instrument by jumping on it in a fit of impotent fury in 1967. The song had too many verses and it took about five years to sort out the right ones.[13]

THE LAW
Various Positions (1985)

One of the differences between Christianity and Judaism is the significance of the Torah, also known as the Pentateuch or the Five Books of Moses. It is the defining text of Judaism, but for Christianity it ranks no higher than any other book in the Bible. Christianity rejected many of the Torah's ritual laws: forbidden foods, circumcision and the biblical festivals, to name just a few. Scholars continue to debate the question, but a common view is that Christianity has by and large rejected 'the Law', as the Torah is frequently called in the New Testament.[14]

Cohen was profoundly touched by Christianity. He saw it as 'the great missionary arm of Judaism'. He explained in a poem that growing up in Montreal was a Christian experience: 'We who belong to this city have never left the Church.' Every aspect of Montreal life, including the Jews, he continues, is in the church. As a child he was regularly taken to church by his Irish Catholic nanny, and he once said that he was brought up 'part Catholic in a certain way'.[15] His manager, Robert Kory, recalled that Cohen always wore a bracelet with images of the great Catholic saints.[16]

But Christianity's appeal to Cohen did not extend to a rejection of the Law. In one of his least-known songs, recorded on his 1985 album *Various Positions*, he sings '**There's a Law, there's an Arm, there's a Hand**'. In the lyrics printed on the album cover the nouns are all capitalized. He is not talking about any old law, arm or hand; he is talking about the Torah, and about the Arm and Hand of God.

> **How many times did you call me**
> **And I knew it was late,**
> **I left everybody**
> **But I never went straight**
> **I don't claim to be guilty**
> **But I do understand**
> **There's a Law, there's an Arm, there's a Hand.**

The Law is a song of regret, in which he makes a confession. Not that he was guilty, but he understands that he had fallen short. He had not gone straight, had not aligned his actions with his desire to return. He had failed to appreciate the Law, failed to obey it.

The Law that Cohen failed to obey, the Law that he now acknowledges, is not the rational but rigorous formalism of the Judaism he grew up with. His Law is the law of the Bible. The biblical God has emotions; he gets angry, he shows compassion, he can be kind or vengeful. He has an Arm and a Hand. The God of the Bible works his wonders as if he has a human body, except of course his body is infinitely powerful – he brought Israel out of Egypt 'with a strong hand and an outstretched arm'.[17] The anthropomorphism by which the Bible describes God was rejected by later Judaism, its philosophers insisting that such descriptions should not be taken literally. But the anthropomorphic

God is the one that Cohen is singing of, the God who has an Arm and a Hand.

> **It wasn't for nothing**
> **That they put me away**
> **I fell with my angel**
> **Down the chain of command**
> **There's a Law, there's an Arm, there's a Hand.**

As the song ends, Cohen offers a further insight into what went wrong. Although he hadn't claimed to be guilty, he knew that he was not condemned for nothing. His offence was to join the wrong side. Yet again he illustrates his point using the book of Revelation, this time the description of the battle in heaven between the archangel Michael and Satan. Michael defeated Satan and hurled him from heaven, together with his band of angels.

Much has been written on the subject of fallen angels, from the apocalyptic texts of the second and first centuries BCE to Milton's *Paradise Lost* and now Leonard Cohen's *The Law*. Cohen is telling us that his mistake was to ally himself with rebels and dissenters – those whom Michael hurled from heaven in the company of Satan. He fell from heaven with his guardian angel, and he was put away. But he knows the remedy. 'There's a Law, there's an Arm, there's a Hand.'

Cohen's Judaism was a defining aspect of his life and a constant theme, particularly in his later work. But his is a spiritual Judaism, the religion of the psalmist and the prophets rather than the rabbis of the Talmud and Midrash. He doesn't reject the rabbis – he returns to the stories they tell in the Talmud time and again – but he is not particularly enamoured with their interpretation of the Law. He challenges their formalism, their emphasis on the rigid details of religious performance rather than on the spirituality that lies beneath it. In his 1978 collection of poetry *Death of a Lady's Man*, he criticized a rabbinic comment that the essence of Torah is the study of the laws relating to sacrificial birds. He called it an 'infuriating presumption'. Yet he was adamant that his criticism of Jewish formalism in no way detracted from his commitment to the faith he was born into. In a TV interview in 1997 he recalled that, when he went to live in the Zen monastery on Mount Baldy, some people accused him of forsaking his Judaism. He quoted in response from a humorous poem he'd written: 'Anyone who says I am not a Jew is not a Jew.'[18]

INTERLUDE: KATERI TEKAKWITHA

Leonard Cohen's 1966 novel *Beautiful Losers* revolves around the seductive appeal of the mysterious Mohawk saint Kateri Tekakwitha. Cohen was fascinated by her. When he lived at the Chelsea Hotel in New York, he would climb the steps of St Patrick's Cathedral on Fifth Avenue, to bind a lily with an elastic band on to the braids of her bronze statue standing in a niche on the door. He used to carry a picture of her in his wallet and had another on the wall of his Montreal house, alongside a photo of another of his great spiritual influences, his teacher Roshi.

Kateri, or Catherine, Tekakwitha was the first First Nation person to be canonized as a saint. She was born around the year 1656, to an Algonquin mother who had been captured by a Mohawk chief. She grew up in a Mohawk village near what is now Albany, New York. When she was four years old, her entire family contracted smallpox. She was the only one to survive, left as an orphan, and with a face badly scarred from the plague. She found her injuries so humiliating that it is said she would wrap her head in a blanket to avoid been stared at.

Alone and different from everyone else, she lived the life of an outsider in the village. It wasn't until she was in her teens that her life began to change, when three Jesuit missionaries arrived to preach to the villagers. She listened carefully to what they had to say and found herself attracted to the idea of Christianity. This didn't go down well in the village; she was persecuted for her growing interest in the Christian faith, and at the age of 20 she ran away. Over a period of several weeks she walked 200 miles, heading for a Christian First Nation mission near Montreal. The missionaries baptized her and gave her the name Catherine. Once she was baptized she took a vow of perpetual virginity. 'The Iroquois are and were a lusty, energetic people,' Leonard Cohen told an interviewer, 'and the fact that she took an oath of virginity was considered very significant.'[19]

Catherine, or Kateri, as her name was pronounced by the Mohawks, was a sickly young woman. She died just five years after her conversion, at the age of 24 or 25. Over the following centuries accounts were written of her life, emphasizing her suffering, her kindness and her faith. By the 1930s she had become a candidate for beatification, and in 1980 Pope John Paul II proclaimed her blessed. In 2011 she was canonized.

Shortly after her beatification Cohen was asked whether he considered the popular interest in Kateri Tekakwitha as part of a new, developing Canadian narrative. 'I did a lot for that girl,' he replied. 'I was very gratified when someone sent me an Italian newspaper on the day she was beatified and it had an excerpt in Italian from *Beautiful Losers*. I did love the woman.'[20]

His fascination with Kateri Tekakwitha was bolstered by his memory of the trips he took as a young child with his father to the First Nation Reserve near Montreal. They would go on Sunday afternoons to watch the dances. He didn't know anything about her at the time, but when he did grow interested in her, he found it deeply significant that her remains are buried on the Reserve that he and his father would visit.

He said of Kateri Tekakwitha that 'she embodied in her own life, in her own choices, many of the complex things that face us always. She spoke to me. She still speaks to me.' He was referring, among other things, to her decision to turn aside from her traditional tribal culture to set off on a path that had summoned her. Yet she did this without forsaking her own people or her identity, becoming a First Nation saint.[21] Leonard Cohen took a similar, if less dramatic, journey. Reluctant to commit to the full-time demands of the Jewish lifestyle that his parents and grandparents had led, he nevertheless refused to compromise his Jewishness, or his respect and affection for its traditions and values.

Shaar Hashomayim Synagogue, Montreal in Cohen's grandfathers' day. Both his grandfather and great-grandfather had been presidents of the congregation. Cohen attended the synagogue regularly while he was growing up. The synagogue choir can be heard on Cohen's track *It Seemed the Better Way*, on his album *You Want It Darker*.

Leonard Cohen at a party for him and Irving Layton, thrown by publishers McClelland and Stewart at Toronto's Fire Hall Restaurant in 1973. Cohen was surprised to find 300 guests at what he expected to be a private party.

Leonard Cohen and guitar, photographed at his concert in
Paris, 12 May 1970.

Leonard Cohen, Marianne Ihlen and friends, on the Greek island of Hydra, shortly after
Cohen arrived in 1960. He spent several years on Hydra, buying a house there, to which he
returned frequently during his career.

Confrontation on stage, Hamburg 1970, after Cohen provoked the crowd by goose-stepping, lifting his arm and crying 'Sieg Heil'. The crowd erupted in rage, one of them reportedly charging the stage with a gun.

Cohen pictured in 1967 by the renowned celebrity portrait photographer Jack Robinson. Robinson completed hundreds of portrait assignments for *Vogue*, mostly of subjects who were just becoming known on the music scene.

The Chelsea Hotel in New York, home over the decades to dozens of artists, writers and musicians. Cohen stayed there during the 1960s and 1970s. He sang about the hotel on his *New Skin for the Old Ceremony* album.

Cohen in his bare apartment in 1991, before leaving to live at the Mount Baldy monastery, where he studied with his teacher Joshu Sasaki Roshi. Cohen was later ordained as a Buddhist monk himself.

Front cover of *Book of Longing*. Published in 2006, it was Cohen's first book of poetry for 20 years. He said that much of the book was an ironic reflection of the religious vocation.

Leonard Cohen in concert at the O2 Arena, London, 15 September 2013, part of his final world tour. He played over 50 gigs across the world from April to December 2013. He was one year short of his 80th birthday.

Inauguration of Leonard Cohen's art exhibition at Oviedo University in October 2011. The exhibition, which toured the world, included self-portraits, landscapes, portraits of women and iconography sketched and painted throughout Cohen's life.

A mural of Leonard Cohen on a building in Crescent Street, Montreal, Cohen's home town. The 10,000 square-foot mural, entitled 'Tower of Songs' was created by artists Gene Pendon and El Mac and replicates a photo taken by Cohen's daughter Lorca.

DIFFERENT SIDES
Old Ideas (2012)

As far as Leonard Cohen was concerned, the boundaries between Judaism and Christianity are pretty fluid. Unlike priests, rabbis and theologians, he saw no immutable separation between the faiths. But in recognizing so much overlap between the religions he was also conscious of their apparent differences. Differences that, as he shows in *Different Sides*, are often more perceived than real.

Different Sides is the final track on his 2012 album *Old Ideas*. He was 77 years old when the album was released, and although it turned out not to be his final record, he must have wondered whether it might be his swansong. He had come out of retirement a few years earlier, after discovering the theft by his then manager of millions of dollars from his various accounts, trust funds and investments. Cohen was financially ruined, and of an age at which it must have seemed impossible to restore his fortunes. But he didn't give up.

Although he was worried and apprehensive, he listened to the counsel of his friends and advisers and went back on the road. Over the next five years he did three world tours, playing dozens of concerts in Europe, North America and Australia. His final tour, which ran for a year from October 2012, coincided with the release of the *Old Ideas* album. They called it the *Old Ideas* World Tour.

We find ourselves on different sides
Of a line that nobody drew

Though it all may be one in the higher eye,
Down here where we live it is two.

Different Sides is a dialogue between two people, who, as the title implies, find themselves opposed to each other, with a line between them. Nobody has drawn this line; it doesn't really exist. It is just that our flawed human perception is unable to grasp that from the higher perspective there is a unity to everything. We see everything as fragmented, even though it is all one. Each side may consider itself different from the other, but in reality they are both the same.

Many of Leonard Cohen's compositions contain more than one theme, or can be interpreted in more than one way. We can't always be certain whether he is addressing God or a lover, whether his lyrics are about sex or theology, or whether, more probably, he is deliberately blending the two. Procreation, as the Kabbalah asserts, is a holy act.

As he grew older, theological themes became more prominent in his work: 'I was living a kind of hermit's life, which was not altogether disagreeable, for 10 or 15 years ... And a certain distance had developed between me and my work, although I never stopped working, I never stopped writing. But I think the writing took a certain more theological, more philosophical bent.'[22]

We see this philosophical bent in *Different Positions*. The theological differences he sings about are between Christianity and Judaism. He presents us with what we can think of as three riddles, which encapsulate the differences he wants to highlight. The answer to each riddle is a paradox. The point he is making is that, while each faith sees itself as different, in reality whatever we say about one faith can equally be said about the other. In the 'higher eye' we are one.

> **I to my side call the meek and the mild**
> **You to your side call the Word.**

The paradox in this verse is not hard to spot. It is Christianity that extols the virtues of 'the meek and the mild', Judaism that is founded on the divine 'Word' proclaimed at Mount Sinai. But the opposite can also be true.

We know that '**the meek and the mild**' refers to Christianity from the words of Jesus. 'Take my yoke upon you, he counsels, and learn of me; for I am meek and lowly in heart.' Or, in the Sermon on the Mount: 'Blessed are the meek for they will inherit the earth.' Even though these ideas can also be found in Judaism, in the book of Psalms and the description in Numbers of Moses' humility, the imperative of meekness is far more central to Christian thought than it is to Judaism.[23]

It is also evident that Judaism is founded on the idea of words. In the booklet containing the lyrics for *Different Sides*, Cohen wrote '**the Word**' with a capital W. This is no ordinary word. It is the word of God, the Torah, spoken to Moses and relayed to the people. It is the utterances in the first chapter of Genesis through which the world was created. It is the Ten Commandments, a misnomer that should properly be translated from the Hebrew as the Ten Words. 'Hear the Word of the Lord,' thunder the prophets.[24]

But the paradox is that '**the meek and the mild**' can also be understood as referring to Judaism, and '**the Word**' as referring to Christianity. 'In the Beginning was the Word,' says the Gospel of John in its first verse, 'and the Word was with God.' Unlike the Hebrew Bible, John doesn't open with a description of the creation of the world. The gospel starts one stage earlier, when the potential for creation is all that there was. This potential was the Word, the word that was spoken when the process of creation began.

As for 'the meek and the mild', this is how Jews have historically been seen: persecuted and downtrodden, turning the other cheek despite there being no religious obligation for them to do so.

Cohen's first riddle is a paradox. Judaism and Christianity are indistinguishable; the characteristics that apply to one also apply to the other. They may appear to be on different sides. But in the 'higher eye', Cohen says, they are one. The qualities that seem to distinguish them from each other – meekness on the one hand, the Word on the other – can equally be applied to each religion. The different sides turn out to be the same.

> **The pull of the moon the thrust of the sun**
> **And thus the ocean is crossed ...**

The second riddle starts with a double entendre. '**The pull of the moon, the thrust of the sun**' is undoubtedly erotic, the moon, generally regarded as the feminine principle, pulling the thrusting, male sun towards her. But there is also an allusion here to an old Jewish legend, one that Cohen may have come across when studying the Talmud or thumbing through his grandfather's compendium of biblical interpretations, in which it also features.[25] It's a story of two rivalries. One rivalry is between the sun and the moon, the other between Jacob and his twin brother, Esau. Esau, in Jewish mythology, was believed to be the ancestor of Rome, the city where Christianity became a global faith. For the Jews the name of Esau's homeland, Edom, became shorthand for Christianity.

The rivalry between the sun and moon occurred when they were created, one to rule over the day, the other over the night. When God first made them, they were of equal size. The moon objected, saying that it was not possible for two rulers to appear to be the same. 'In that case', said God, 'you can be smaller.'

The moon objected to this, arguing that she was being punished for speaking the truth. 'OK,' said God, 'to make up for it, you can shine during the day as well as the night.' But the moon was still not happy, since the light of the sun would make her almost invisible by day. So, as a further compensation, God said that Jacob and his descendants would count the months by the moon, each month beginning whenever the moon was new. And to make things fair, the descendants of Jacob's brother Esau, symbolizing Christianity, would use the sun to calculate their year.[26]

The purpose of the legend is to explain why the Jewish calendar is based on the moon, and the Christian on the sun.

In a lunar calendar each month begins with the new moon. In the solar calendar the 365 days that the earth takes to rotate around the sun are divided into 12 months of roughly equal lengths. When Cohen sings of the sun and moon, he is singing of Judaism and Christianity.

There is a paradox here too. For the Jewish calendar is not fully lunar. It is calculated so as to bring the lunar year periodically in line with the solar rotation. And the Christian calendar is not fully solar: the dates of Lent, Easter and Whitsun are calculated by the moon. When Cohen sings of the moon pulling, the sun thrusting, he is describing the tension between the two faiths, illustrated by their apparently different calendars, but the calendars turn out to be not so different after all.

But that is not all. The riddle is more than a legend; there is history in it too. The real reason why the Church uses a solar calendar is that that was the method used in Rome. But the Church calendar also contains an echo of an earlier dispute, from pre-Christian times, between two Jewish sects. One group were the Pharisees, the forerunners of modern Judaism. The other was a group we know little about, among whom were the people who wrote the Dead Sea Scrolls. They argued over the calendar.

Calendar disputes are important because social harmony is so much easier to achieve if everyone celebrates the holidays, festivals and sabbaths at the same time. But these two groups could not agree. The Pharisees insisted on a lunar calendar. The other group calculated their dates by the sun, dividing the

365 days of the year into 12 equal portions of 30 days each. They added in extra days periodically, to make up the number of 365 days in the solar year.

This solar calendar was mathematically harmonious; its holy days fell on the same day of the week each year, always on Sundays, Wednesdays or Fridays. And although the dates of Easter, Lent and Whitsun are based on when the first full moon falls in spring, the days of the week on which they invariably fall come from the ancient pre-Christian solar calendar: Whit Sunday, Ash Wednesday and Good Friday.

So there's the paradox. The lunar calendar that is part solar. And the solar calendar that is part lunar. Down here, where we live, the calendars appear different. But from above they look the same.

The Pharisees feature in the third riddle too: '**And thus the ocean is crossed**.' The Pharisees were one of the two dominant Jewish sects at the time, made up mainly of scholars and working people. In the Gospels, Matthew rebuked them, saying they would even traverse the ocean to make a convert: 'Woe to you, scribes and Pharisees, hypocrites! For you travel land and sea to win one proselyte, and when he is won, you make him twice as much a son of hell as yourselves.'[27]

The paradox is that Matthew's rebuke to the Pharisees was written at exactly the time when Christianity was actively proselytizing: attracting converts by spreading its influence northwards into Syria and Asia Minor, sailing across the Mediterranean to Rome. The two faiths crossing the waters in tandem, the sun of Christianity thrusting, the moon of Judaism pulling, each seeking out new adherents; their boundaries fluid and conjoined.

... The waters are blessed while a shadowy guest Kindles a light for the lost

Now that he has shown that the differences between the faiths are not as ingrained as it may appear, Cohen turns to a divergence that is not so easily reconciled. It begins at birth, when a new-born child is initiated into the faith of its parents. A baby is welcomed into Christianity through baptism with holy water, 'waters' that 'are blessed'. And baby boys are initiated into Judaism through circumcision. These rites are not so easily reconciled.

A long-established Jewish tradition is to place a chair for the prophet Elijah at a circumcision ritual. According to the Bible, Elijah did not die. He ascended to heaven in a fiery chariot. Legend has it that he continues to roam the world, usually unseen. One day he will reveal himself to announce the coming of the Messiah. Until then he is a shadowy figure, turning up as a guest at every circumcision, perhaps checking to see if this is the child he will proclaim as the Saviour.

What does Cohen have him do, this shadowy guest? He kindles a light for the lost, for the vanished and dead. As in so much of Cohen's music, there is a darkness in *Different Sides*. He alludes to it in the chorus: '**Both of us say there are laws to obey, But frankly I don't like your tone.**' Having pointed out their similarities, Cohen reminds us that there has been conflict between the two faiths, historically even if not now. That conflict was thrown into sharpest focus by the Shoah, the Holocaust, the culmination of centuries of European persecution of the Jews. It is for the victims of the Shoah and other evils that the shadowy guest kindles a light.

Different Sides shows us that the differences between Christianity and Judaism are insubstantial. But they nevertheless stand on different sides. However much dialogue and reconciliation there is today between the faiths, we cannot escape the tragedies of history and the ongoing conflicts of human life.

We are done with theology. The remainder of the song deals with the broken world that Cohen sees all around him — famine, suffering, broken relationships and strife. We are into different themes, beyond the scope of this book. But the differences are not all they seem; in the higher eye they are all one.

IT SEEMED THE BETTER WAY
You Want It Darker (2016)

Throughout his career Leonard Cohen drew freely on both Christian and Jewish sources, rarely differentiating or seeing a dividing line between them. He seemed to be as knowledgeable about the Christian faith as about the Judaism he was born into. He recognized the sanctity of Christianity, and he esteemed Christ as highly as he did any character from the Jewish tradition.

> I don't think in all of human history there has been a person who has so closely identified himself with the downtrodden, the outsiders, the victims, criminals, prostitutes. [28]

Cohen's admiration for Christ may explain why he did not share the fearful antipathy of many Jews towards Christianity, a view they considered vindicated by centuries of persecution culminating in the Holocaust. Unlike some of his peers he saw Christianity in a positive light, as a product of Jewish ideas, a faith designed to disseminate the values of the Judaism that Jesus practised:

> I love Christ. I see Christianity as the world historic mission of certain ideas that the Jews developed. Christianity is a mighty movement, and that is the way those ideas penetrated the world. Christianity is the missionary arm

of Judaism. As Maimonides said, 'We're all working for the world to come.'[29]

Only occasionally did he express reservations about Christianity. Jennifer Warnes, his long-term collaborator and backing singer, recalled that when Bob Dylan converted to Christianity in 1979, Cohen would 'wander around the house, wringing his hands, saying "I don't get it. I just don't get this. Why would he go for Jesus at a late time like this? I don't get the Jesus part."'[30]

Yet, if we are to take the song *It Seemed the Better Way* at face value, the thought of embracing Christianity does seem to have appealed to Leonard Cohen at some stage in his life, possibly when he was much younger.

It seemed the better way
When first I heard him speak
But now it's much too late
To turn the other cheek
Sounded like the truth
… But it's not the truth today.

It Seemed the Better Way is the penultimate track on *You Want It Darker*, the final album that Cohen issued before he died. It is a hymn rather than a song. The music was written by Patrick Leonard, who produced several of Cohen's later albums. Behind Cohen's voice we hear the choir of Montreal's Shaar Hashomayim synagogue, the synagogue where he grew up, where his grandfather and great-grandfather had been presidents. The choir's harmonies are eerily reminiscent of the music of the Day of the Atonement – the song could almost be interpreted as a confession.

There is not much in the song that tells us Cohen is singing about the possibility of converting to Christianity. The only hints are the line in the first verse – '**it's much too late, to turn the other cheek**' – and the final couplet evoking the Sacrament: '**Lift this glass of blood, Try to say the grace**.' Without these, it could be a song about any ideology or faith that Cohen was contemplating signing up to.

But like many of his songs, *It Seemed the Better Way* went through many revisions before it was finally recorded. In an earlier version, one that was never published but which he made available to the Leonard Cohen Files website, we read that only a '**fool would bless the meek today**', and that he wonders what is meant by '**This rising up with love, This lying down with death**.'

It Seemed the Better Way leaves us with unanswered questions: when did Christianity seem to Cohen to be a better way? And why does it no longer sound like the truth?

Perhaps we can find the answer by comparing his line '**It's much too late to turn the other cheek**' with his reaction to Bob Dylan's conversion, 'Why would he go for Jesus at a late time like this?' Many years earlier he had spoken of seeing himself as the 'cantor in a catacomb religion', a new underground faith for the times we live in. He was saying that the old religions had served their time; their ideas may still have had value, but as institutions their day had passed. Had he not been born a Jew, he would almost certainly not have converted to Judaism. He might have done so 2,000 years earlier, when the religion was still fresh and vital. But not now. The same applied to Christianity. Once, becoming a Christian might have seemed the better way. But not now, not in the twenty-first century. Not after history had made it impossible '**to turn the other cheek**'. It was much too late.

4

HEAVEN AND EARTH

The Bible says very little about the secrets of heaven. The prophet Ezekiel had a vision of the heavenly throne, and Isaiah visited the divine abode, but neither gave much detail about what goes on up there, or how it affects our life on earth.

A dramatic description of life in heaven comes from the book of Revelation, written several hundred years after Isaiah and Ezekiel prophesied. Revelation is an apocalyptic text; part visionary, part prophesy, it is packed with graphic, detailed accounts of heaven, with fearsome revelations of things to come and descriptions of apocalyptic events that will usher in the end of time. It belongs to a genre of literature that flourished roughly between 200 BCE and 100 CE, books full of angels and demons, dire predictions and terrifying happenings. Revelation itself is thought to have been written towards the end of this period, during the latter half of the first century CE.

Cohen was particularly enamoured of Revelation. Along with the *I Ching* and *The Tibetan Book of the Dead*, Revelation was one of the ancient works that he would discuss with his friends when living on the island of Hydra.

> So, the Book of Revelation is a kind of manual. It's wonderful poetry and it's wonderful revelation and it certainly does fulfil that great characteristic of charged writing by pulling the rug out from under you, and you are in a new world, and there is a new Jerusalem, and you are ready to embrace the notion of newness and rebirth and of a new cosmos, and it invites you to unfold that reality in your own heart and in your own life, that dissolving of time.[1]

Round about the time that Revelation was written, Jewish mystics began to think more deeply about Ezekiel's vision of the heavenly throne. They were keen to draw closer to God, to experience what the prophet had experienced and to visit heaven for themselves. Gradually they developed theories about the mystical relationship between heaven and earth, about the process of creation and the divine nature of the human soul. They drew heavily on Greek philosophy, particularly the discipline known as Neoplatonism. Neoplatonists held, among other things, that the whole of existence emanated in stages from a single source, and that each stage was caused by the one above it and in turn generated a lower stage below. By the twelfth century the Jewish mystics had a name for their Neoplatonic system. They called it Kabbalah.

Leonard Cohen knew much about Kabbalah and frequently used its imagery in his lyrics. He didn't speak about it often;

Kabbalah is not a subject that lends itself to casual conversation. Once, however, when he was playing in Jerusalem, he was so stoned that he couldn't perform properly and felt he was letting the audience down. He told them that he couldn't get off the ground, and that the Kabbalah says if you can't get off the ground, you shouldn't try. (The audience didn't seem to mind too much; he did manage to get off the ground eventually, and played.)

One of the recurring themes in Leonard Cohen's music is that of brokenness. Hearts, hills, nights, thrones, banjos, people, feelings, families – they are all broken at one time or another. Cohen sees the world as broken, in need of repair. And although this is probably a reflection of his own melancholic tendencies, it chimes very neatly with a key idea in Kabbalah, that something went wrong at the moment when the world was created, leaving divine sparks scattered about the earth, embers that need to be gathered up and restored to their rightful place. Cohen expands on this idea in several songs. In *It's Torn*, which was released in 2019 on his posthumous album *Thanks for the Dance*, he constructs a series of metaphors, some kabbalistic, some mundane, all showing how the very fabric of creation has been sundered. His remedy is to 'Come gather the pieces all scattered and lost'.

The Kabbalists maintain that the cosmos, the spiritual universe, is composed of two halves, each mirroring the other. The dominant half, the one that will ultimately prevail, is on the right-hand side; it is the domain of all that is good. Opposite it is the domain of evil. It is called, somewhat unimaginatively, 'the other side'. Cohen sometimes found himself there. 'I greet you from the other side', he sings in *Heart with No Companion*. The other side, he tells us, is one of despair, one in which his vast love has been shattered. But all is not gloom; the love of which he sings will ultimately reach everywhere. As he sang in *Anthem,* a song we will discuss shortly, 'There is a crack in everything. That's how the light gets in.'

YOU KNOW WHO I AM
Songs from a Room (1969)

On 28 August 1970, on his first European tour, after the débâcle in Hamburg and two days before he calmed the crowd at the Isle of Wight Festival, Cohen gave a concert at the Henderson Hospital near London. The hospital was a residential therapeutic centre for people with severe psychological difficulties. He told his audience that the song he was about to play 'had something to do with some 300 acid trips I took'. The song was *You Know Who I Am*.[2]

If it is in the nature of acid trips to garb simple truths in dazzling, beguiling fantasies, then *You Know Who I Am* was undoubtedly the product of Cohen's fondness for LSD. *You Know Who I Am* is among the most cryptic of his works, yet the idea that it conveys could hardly be simpler. Drawing on the Bible and Kabbalah, Cohen's poetic metaphor is about the unknowability of God.

> **You know who I am**
> **You've stared at the sun**
> **Well I am the one who loves**
> **Changing from nothing to one.**

He was the one who had stared at the sun, he mysteriously told his producer, Bob Johnston, when he asked him why he wanted to perform in a mental hospital. He told Johnston that he had taken a lot of LSD, gone out in a little boat and stared at the sun too long.[3]

In *You Know Who I Am* Cohen is being addressed by God, who gave his name as *I am* when he appeared to Moses at the Burning Bush. When Moses asked who he was, God replied: 'I am what I am; thus you shall say to the Israelites: "I am sent me to you".'[4] But Cohen is being told in the song that 'I am' is also 'the one who loves changing from nothing to one'. *I am* may be a name of God. But the manifestation of God that we perceive, according to the Kabbalah, is his unity, when he mystically transitions from nothing to one. As we will see, it's a complex idea, which Cohen has summed up in a few inscrutable words.

The Kabbalah maintains that God cannot be described in words. He is beyond all definition. If we try to describe him, he becomes constrained by our description. When we define God, it is as if we imply that he is limited by the words we use to describe him. God can only be God if he defies definition, if he is beyond all limit, greater than anything that can possible be conceived. The Kabbalah refers to God as *ein sof,* 'without end' – he is both everything and nothing.

Yet those of a religious sensibility believe that they can perceive God. Kabbalah tries to explain how this can be – how something so indescribable can touch people's lives, can even create a material world.

To explain this, Kabbalah resorts to metaphor. The cosmos can be described as a tree, with a top, a root and branches in between. It can also be pictured as the body of a person, with a head, feet and limbs. The image is variously called the Tree of Life, or Primordial Man. In this metaphor the infinite aspect of God that we call 'without end' lies in the emptiness beyond the top of the tree. Infinitely vast, yet impossibly small, *ein sof* is beyond any conception that we can have of existence. This is the 'nothing' of *You Know Who I Am*: the 'changing from nothing to one'. This is the God that is beyond all perception.

Conversely, the foundation of Jewish belief lies in a simple, one-line statement that summarizes our knowledge of God. Known as the *Shema*, it comes from the book of Deuteronomy: 'The Lord our God, the Lord is One'. This is the aspect of God that we can perceive, God as One, as an indivisible unity perceived at the root of the Tree of Life, in the region that the kabbalists call the Kingdom, where the spiritual meets the material.

The process by which God descends the tree, changing from nothing to one, is beyond all human comprehension. For hundreds of years, thousands of kabbalists have written millions of words trying to explain it. It makes no sense to most of us, and although Leonard Cohen probably had a better intuitive grasp of it than most people, the process is far beyond the realms of his song. All we need to know is that the *I am* of the Burning Bush, God who appeared and spoke to Moses, is the same God who revealed himself to Cohen on his acid trips, as he stared at the sun. It is the God whom Kabbalah tries to explain, whom Cohen sums up in his pithy line '**The one who loves changing from nothing to one**'. From the infinite nothingness of *ein sof* to the unity of God in the world.

The phrase is implicitly circular. Starting with one, becoming nothing then changing to one. This circularity, we shall see, is significant for the way in which Leonard Cohen has constructed his song.

I cannot follow you, my love, you cannot follow
  me …

God may have revealed himself to Cohen, but there is an unbridgeable gap between them. In the opening verse God emphasizes just how vast this gap is. That God cannot follow Cohen goes without saying; he addresses Cohen as '**my love**', almost condescendingly, as if to emphasize the absurdity of thinking otherwise. But nor, says God, is Cohen able to follow him. It reflects a failing on Cohen's part. 'You shall follow the Lord your God', says the book of Deuteronomy; but Cohen does not have the ability. There is too much distance between them, he explains in the next line, and God himself is that distance, placed there by Cohen whenever he fails to commune with the Almighty.

But God is not so remote, we are told in the second verse, that he cannot have a relationship with us. We have a partnership with God; he needs us just as we need him. He makes demands on humanity, needing us for his own purposes. Speaking to Cohen in his capacity as a proxy for all of us, God tells him what he requires.

Sometimes I need you naked
Sometimes I need you wild
I need you to carry my children in
And I need you to kill a child.

The demands that God imposes on the human race began in the Garden of Eden, where Adam and Eve were told not to eat from the Tree of Knowledge. Tempted by the snake, they did eat from it, realized that they were naked and covered themselves with fig leaves. Of course, God knew this would happen; the point of the story is to explain the evolution of humanity into sapient creatures. God needed them naked in order that they would learn.

But the story as told in the Bible contains a question that God asks, a question that leads us to conclude that he needs us just as we need him. 'The Lord God called out to the man and said to him, "Where are you?"' The medieval commentator Rashi, drawing on the Talmud, suggests that God wanted to start a conversation. After all, God knows everything, he knew where Adam was, he didn't need to ask him. He called Adam in order to hear him respond. Later philosophers expanded on this idea, of God needing people. They developed the idea of a divine–human partnership. There will be times in this partnership, Cohen continues, when God will need people to be wild, or to carry a child.[5]

But just when God's demands on humanity seem fairly straightforward, Cohen confounds us. He returns us to the trauma of his *Story of Isaac*, which appeared on the same album as *You Know Who I Am*. God's dark warning to Cohen that he may be needed to kill a child leads us in to the third verse and its inevitable question. What sort of being is this God who can make such demands? Who both needs us in our Edenic innocence yet expects us to defy our most basic instincts, simply to test our faith in him?

We can only answer these questions if we approach and confront God, demanding a response from him. But before he can even start looking for God, Cohen receives a further communication: '**If you should ever track me down, I will surrender there**.' Should we ever achieve knowledge of the unknowable, God tells Cohen, he will give way to humankind.

Although he hasn't spelled it out, Cohen is reprising the conversation in the Bible between God and someone, we don't know who, after Adam and Eve ate from the Tree of Knowledge. 'And the Lord God said: "Behold, man has become like one of us, knowing good and evil. And now, lest he stretch out his hand and takes also from the Tree of Life, and lives for ever."'

When they ate from the Tree of Knowledge, Adam and Eve opened the gates of moral awareness. They became ethical beings. Unlike the animals, they now knew the difference between and good and bad; they were capable of evil, just as they were capable of being good. But God feared what might follow. Should they also eat from the tree of immortal life, they would, God says, be 'like one of us'; they would become immortal, all-knowing beings. That's why he threw them out of the Garden of Eden, to prevent them from reaching a spiritual level from which they could challenge God's power. Hence God's message to Cohen: track me down by all means, and I will surrender. But to track God down would require a profound change in Cohen's spiritual nature, one equivalent to returning to the Garden of Eden and eating from the Tree of Life. He would need to achieve a spiritual elevation, a closeness to God, greater than anything anyone has ever accomplished.

The idea of drawing close to God also occurs in Kabbalah. A mystical exercise for many kabbalists is to elevate their souls to a level of spiritual purity from which they can cleave wholeheartedly to God. Getting to such a level requires many weeks of fasting, meditation, mystical gymnastics and the recitation of complex incantations. It is an aspiration fraught with danger, a goal to be pursued by only the most mystically accomplished of initiates. The further one elevates oneself from the rootedness of the material world, the greater the risk of not returning safely. It is this danger of which God now warns Cohen, in the conclusion of the verse.

> **I will leave with you one broken man**
> **Whom I will teach you to repair.**

God will surrender, should Cohen ever track him down. But it will leave Cohen broken. It's not a threat; the brokenness need not be fatal. For, God tells Cohen, he will teach him the remedy, show him how to repair.

The idea of repair is fundamental to the kabbalistic system. Suffused with evil, the world we live in is broken, damaged in the cosmic catastrophe at the moment of creation, which Cohen will sing about many years later in his mystical song *Anthem*. Kabbalists know many formulae, incantations and mystical exercises that can be used to repair the world, heal souls and rectify all types of mortal and spiritual ailments. Tracking God down, cleaving to him, will leave Cohen a broken man. But God will teach him how to perform the repair.

And that brings us full circle. Repaired, Cohen will once again be rooted in the world, remote from God, unable to cleave to him, staring at the sun, searching for the *I Am*. And so as the song ends we return to the first verse: '**I cannot follow you, my love, you cannot follow me …**'

Cohen and God cannot follow each other. We are back where we started. The circularity of '**the one who loves changing from nothing to one**' is reprised in the journey from distance to search to distance again.

ANTHEM
The Future (1992)

Leonard Cohen described *Anthem* as one of the best songs he had ever written, maybe the best. Few of Leonard Cohen's songs contain as much religious symbolism; rarely does he draw from such a wide range of sources. The name itself hints at the song's religious character; deriving from the Greek *antiphon*, in early English the word 'anthem' was used to describe a sacred musical composition.

> **The birds they sang**
> **At the break of day**
> **Start again**
> **I heard them say.**

That birds can deliver messages should come as no surprise to anyone who has read the biblical book of Ecclesiastes. Be careful, Ecclesiastes says, about what you say, because a 'bird of heaven may carry [your] voice, and a winged creature may report your word'.[6] We never know when a bird may be listening.

King Solomon, in both Jewish and Islamic tradition, is said to have been able to understand the language of the birds. The same tradition says that he was the author of Ecclesiastes, although that view is not accepted by modern scholars.

Ecclesiastes is a deeply introspective book. There is nothing like it in the Bible. The author of the book, whoever he was, is searching for the meaning of life. He composes deeply depressing passages describing the pointlessness of life; everything he says is 'vanity', vapid and without meaning. Yet life is not always futile; the book is also optimistic. Eat, drink and gain pleasure from your labour, the author says, 'for I have seen that this too is from the hand of God'.[7]

Ecclesiastes could have been written for Leonard Cohen, prone to deep bouts of depression yet enjoying the pleasures of this world. Explaining why he chose to spend much of his life in the Mount Baldy monastery, he told an interviewer:

> Depression has been an issue with me for the whole of my life and I've tried, like everybody else, various ways of dealing with that depression. You know, drugs, women, art, religion … you try everything … Depression isn't just the blues. It's not just like I've a hangover for the weekend … it's a kind of mental violence which stops you from functioning properly from one moment to the next. You lose something somewhere and suddenly you're gripped by a kind of angst of the heart and of the spirit … I've had to deal with this most of my life like many other people and I've finally found a place like this where there are a lot of people like me.[8]

As in so much of his music, in *Anthem* Cohen is trying to make sense of the world. Both he and the author of Ecclesiastes are on a quest for meaning, to make sense of the paradoxes, the inconsistencies, the apparent futility, of the world.

Part of the solution that Ecclesiastes offers to a life of futility and transient pleasure is to recognize that we live in a world of constant change, to realize that everything repeats, that cosmic occurrences follow a cyclical pattern. It is the message that Cohen heard the birds sing. There is no point in worrying about what has gone before. '**Start again**.' Or, as Ecclesiastes puts it:

> One generation goes, another comes, but the earth remains forever. The sun rises, and the sun sets and returns back to where it rises. The wind goes to the south and turns to the north, turning continually, it returns to its circuits. All the rivers run into the sea, yet the sea is never full; to the place where they go, there they go again ... That which was will be, and that which was done will be done. There is nothing new under the sun.[9]

The message that the birds deliver is that Cohen should seek a new beginning. Start again, they tell him, don't dwell on the past, or on the future. The message is unequivocal: live in the present, treat each day as it comes, make the most of each moment.

This evokes a verse in Isaiah: 'Do not remember the first things, nor consider the matters of old.'[10] In his youth Cohen studied the book of Isaiah with his grandfather, Rabbi Solomon Klonitzky-Kline.

> I remember sitting with my grandfather, studying the book of Isaiah. He was already well along in his years, and he'd read

a passage, and he'd speak about it, and nod off, and his finger would go back to the beginning of the passage as he moved his body, and he'd start fresh, with that same verse again and read it again and expound it again, and sometimes the whole evening was spent on the exposition of one verse.[11]

Flying between heaven and earth, the Kabbalah imagines birds to be a conduit for the divine presence. They bear God's words from the celestial heights to those able to hear them below. They are even shaped like the letters in the divine name. Their head, body and two wings are, according to the Zohar, each fashioned in the shape of one of the letters in God's four-lettered Name. In mystical imagery this Name is the central pillar of the cosmos, the column connecting heaven and earth, the firmament through which the birds fly.[12]

The Gospels also attach a special status to birds, though they single out one species in particular. After Jesus had been baptized, he saw the heavens open. He watched as the Spirit of God, in the form of a dove, descended to earth and alighted on him.[13] The Holy Ghost, conveyed from heaven to earth on the wings of a dove. She too, Cohen tells us, will be caught up in the futilities of which Ecclesiastes speaks. In her case the dove, the symbol of peace, will be caught up in the futility of war. As Ecclesiastes tells us, there is a time for war, and a time for peace.[14]

Ah the wars they will be fought again.
The holy dove she will be caught again.
Bought and sold, and bought again, the dove is
    never free.

War is one of the futilities of life. We have seen that for Leonard Cohen war was an essential aspect of the human condition. Although he rarely commented publicly on world events, war was rarely far from the surface of his concerns. As a child, he had wanted to attend Canada's military academy; he wanted to fight in a war and win medals as his father had done. War is never-ending; true to the cyclical pattern disclosed by Ecclesiastes, all wars will be fought again. The holy dove too will be caught again.

The dove occupies a special place in biblical tradition. Although it may offend our sensibilities, the dove, along with its cousin the pigeon, was the only bird sufficiently sacred to be offered as a sacrifice in the ancient Jerusalem temple. But that is not why the Holy Dove alighted on Jesus after his baptism. The fact that it was a sacrificial victim is unlikely to have qualified the dove to be the instrument on which the Holy Ghost was borne. The dove's pre-eminence goes back to the story of Noah's Ark, where it was the saviour of humanity. Had the dove not flown back to Noah carrying an olive leaf in its beak, from which he deduced that the flood waters had sunk beneath the tops of the trees, the old man and his family might have never emerged from the ark and the human race may not have survived.

In both the Gospels and the story of Noah the dove is a divine messenger, an instrument of salvation. In the Gospels it conveyed the Holy Ghost to Jesus, whereupon a heavenly voice announced: 'This is my son, whom I love; with him I am well pleased.' In the Hebrew Bible it gave corrupt humanity a second chance after the waters of the flood had swept the former generations to oblivion.[15]

Yet the dove only plays a minor part in the Noah narrative. Many years later another biblical author decided that the dove needed to be given greater credit for saving the world. He composed an allegory in which the dove was cast in the role of an obscure Hebrew prophet. This prophet, like Noah's dove, had been sent on a mission of salvation; his job was to give a second chance to the wicked people in the Assyrian capital, Nineveh. The storyteller gave the prophet a narrative as fabulous and unbelievable as that of Noah's Ark.

Like the dove, the prophet was sent on a mission. Unlike the dove, he didn't want to go. He fled to a port and boarded a ship. He was caught in a storm, thrown overboard by the sailors and swallowed by a giant fish. Like the dove, he traversed the waters until he found dry land. Spewed from the fish's belly, he resumed his mission, travelling to the city of Nineveh, where, like the dove, he delivered his omen of salvation.

The prophet's name of course was Jonah – *Yonah* in Hebrew. *Yonah* is the Hebrew word for 'dove'. '**Bought and sold, and bought again, the dove is never free**.' Jonah the dove, lurching from crisis to crisis; the Holy Spirit, incarnate, crucified and resurrected; the cycle of recurring events echoing Ecclesiastes.

Anthem took Cohen a decade to write. During this time it went through many different iterations. It is, he told an interviewer, a reflection on the flaws of humanity, on our imperfections. But, as he explains in the chorus, 'it is by intimacy with the flaw that we discern our real humanity and our real connection with divine inspiration.'[16]

> **Ring the bells that still can ring**
> **Forget your perfect offering**
> **There is a crack in everything**
> **That's how the light gets in.**

In a broken world, in which our spirituality, our connection with what is beyond, has become as flawed as everything else, even the church bells have, for the main part, fallen silent. Ringing those bells that can still be rung is an act of defiance, a statement that we will not give in to the brokenness of everything; it is the theme that runs through all four lines of the chorus.

'The future is no excuse for an abdication of your own personal responsibilities, towards yourself and your job and your love,' Cohen told an interviewer in 1992. "**Ring the bells that still can ring**": they're few and far between, but you can find them.'

> This situation does not admit a solution of perfection. This is not the place where you make things perfect, neither in your marriage, nor in your work, nor anything, nor your love of God, nor your love of family or country. The thing is imperfect.
>
> And worse, there is a crack in everything that you can put together: physical objects, mental objects, constructions of any kind. But that's where the light gets in, and

that's where the resurrection is and that's where the return,
that's where the repentance is. It is with the confrontation,
with the brokenness of things.[17]

Other, even older bells have also fallen silent. Cohen, as a
cohen, of the ancient priestly family, was undoubtedly aware
of them. The book of Exodus describes the clothes that were
to be made for Cohen's ancestor, Aaron the High Priest,
when he ministered in the Sanctuary. Among them was a
kaftan of pure blue wool. Around the hem were pomegranate
tassels made of blue, purple and crimson yarns. Between
the pomegranates were golden bells. The bells tinkled
as the High Priest walked, trilling as he officiated in the
Sanctuary. When the Temple in Jerusalem was destroyed,
the High Priest's bells fell silent. These too are bells that
can no longer ring, bells that were part of Leonard Cohen's
priestly heritage.

When the priestly bells can't ring, the perfect offering can't
be sacrificed. The perfect offering is Jesus, as the Epistle to the
Hebrews explains when discussing his sacrifice on the cross:
'For by one offering he has perfected for all time those who
are sanctified.'[18] In offering himself, Jesus brought salvation to
others.

The idea of Jesus as a sacrifice for the salvation of the world
underpins Christian theology. But in a flawed world, says
Cohen, one cannot rely on the perfection of Jesus' sacrifice on
the cross. As in his first verse, Cohen's message is that we have
to make the most of what we've got. Don't dwell on the past

or on the future, the ideal is no longer attainable. 'Forget the perfect offering.'

Leonard Cohen described arguably his most famous two lines, '**There is a crack in everything, That's how the light gets in**' as 'the closest thing I could describe to a credo. That idea is one of the fundamental positions behind a lot of the songs.'[19]

A succinct juxtaposition of despair and optimism, the couplet was described by a distinguished professor of Kabbalah as Leonard Cohen's most paramount kabbalistic declaration.[20] It is based on a creation myth expounded by the sixteenth-century kabbalistic master Isaac Luria. Widely regarded as the most innovative and influential of all kabbalists, Luria developed his mystical philosophy in the kabbalistic fraternity in Safed, northern Israel, where he spent the last three years of his short life.

Luria's creation myth attempts to explain how God created the cosmos. If God was all that existed, where could he place the physical universe? There was apparently no space outside of him where the world could be sited. And anyway, how could God, a wholly ethereal being with no physical aspect to him, create a material world? These were very real problems in an early modern world where religion and science still overlapped, where it was still possible for questions of cause and effect to have a mystical dimension.

Luria's solution was based on the concept of *tzimtzum*, withdrawal. God created space for the universe by contracting his essence, withdrawing himself into himself, leaving behind a void in which creation could take place. Yet, empty of God's presence, the void was not completely vacant. Negative forces were left behind, forces that had originally been diluted and rendered insignificant by the vast expanse of divine light, but which now coalesced into a dense mass. From this mass the concrete, physical worlds, emerged. Negative in nature, the material worlds were lifeless, chaotic and unformed: they were the shapeless chaos described at the beginning of Genesis.[21]

Genesis tells us that God's first utterance was 'Let there be light'. In Luria's myth this was a ray of divine light that shot into the void he had created, animating the mass of negative energy and infusing it with spiritual vitality. The light expanded, forming itself into the shape of a human being, known as Primordial Adam. Beams of light burst forth from the eyes of Primordial Adam, collecting into ten vessels constructed out of the negative energy that had remained in the void. The vessels were arranged in a hierarchy, those above being closer to the divine source of all, those beneath them progressively influencing the cosmos that was beginning to materialize below.

But things started to go wrong. As more and more light flowed into the lower vessels, they became increasingly unstable. In a catastrophic eruption they shattered, their fragments and their light spiralling to the earth below. The sparks of divine light landed first, the shells of the vessels composed of negative energy landed on them, smothering them. The shells are still on the ground today; they account for the evil in the world. The sparks concealed beneath them are of divine light, seeking to be reunited with the source from which it was torn.[22]

Luria's Kabbalah obliges us to remove the material covering that conceals the light, so that the sparks can ascend to their rightful place. This is done through the performance of good deeds, correct behaviour, sincere prayer and the fulfilment of biblical commandments. The divine light may be concealed beneath the husks of materialism; good may be smothered by evil. But the shells cannot conceal the light completely; there is always a glimmer of hope. As Leonard Cohen sings,

There is a crack in everything.
That's how the light gets in.

Cohen spoke about the light that gets in in a 1992 interview with TV Ontario:

The light is the capacity to reconcile your experience, your sorrow with every day that dawns. It is that understanding which is beyond significance or meaning, that allows you to live a life and embrace the disasters and sorrows and joys that are our common lot. But it's only with the recognition that there is a crack in everything. I think all other versions are doomed to irretrievable gloom.[23]

As the optimism of the previous verse fades away, Cohen returns to our broken world. The next theme he takes up is the betrayal of the messianic dream. His lyrics in this verse are even more enigmatic and, as always, are capable of more than one interpretation. He begins by singing that we had asked for signs. These signs had been sent, yet a birth had been betrayed and a marriage had been spent. Most enigmatically of all, this has led to the widowhood of every government; all can see these signs:

> We asked for signs, the signs were sent, the birth
> betrayed, the marriage spent;
> Yeah the widowhood of every government – signs
> for all to see.

The most likely sources for this verse are the messianic prophesies in the book of Isaiah, the book Cohen studied in depth with his grandfather. The book tells of a sign that the prophet Isaiah gave to Ahaz, king of Judah, when he was threatened with invasion from the north. Isaiah indicated a woman who was about to give birth. He told the king that the woman would name the child Immanuel and that before he was even old enough to know good from evil, Ahaz's enemies would be defeated.[24]

Two chapters later Isaiah announces that the child has been born. He is given another name; no longer simply Immanuel, the child is now extravagantly named Wonderful Counsellor, Mighty God, Everlasting Father, Prince of Peace. The child, Isaiah tells us, will magnify the authority and peace of the Davidic dynasty, of which Ahaz is a descendant. His government will be founded on justice and equity.[25]

Christianity understands these prophecies as foretelling the birth of Jesus. But Jesus' birth was betrayed, sings Cohen. Not just on the human level, when he was betrayed to the Romans by Judas. Jesus' birth was also betrayed on a cosmic level. The messianic promise of Jesus' birth has been betrayed. Isaiah's assurance of a just and peaceful government did not come to pass. The predicted messianic government has nothing to govern: '**the widowhood of every government**'.

Isaiah's prophecies have a similar interpretation in Jewish tradition, but there the child is not Jesus but King Ahaz's son Hezekiah. According to this view, Hezekiah was supposed to be the Messiah. But he did not live up to expectations. The Talmud portrays a dispute in heaven over whether or not Hezekiah gave thanks properly when his enemies were miraculously defeated. The earth and the angel who oversees the world argued in Hezekiah's favour, stating that, despite his failings, he should still become the Messiah. But the spirit of immaculate justice, which decries any sort of favouritism, was opposed. The divine decree went against him.[26]

In this myth, Hezekiah's failure to become the Messiah was the cause of the decline of the kingdom and the eventual exile of the Jews to Babylon. The prophet Jeremiah, preaching at the time of the exile, described the exile as the failure of Israel's marriage to God. 'I have sent her away and given her a bill of divorce', he has God saying.[27] The messianic kingdom had not been established, the marriage between God and Israel was spent. '**The widowhood of every government**.'

The structure of *Anthem* is a repeating pattern of two verses followed by a chorus, or antiphon. The first verses, preceding the first antiphon, are based loosely on Ecclesiastes. They deal with the circular nature of existence and the quest for meaning. Verses three and four also constitute a unit; they both deal with a flawed and mismanaged world.

> **I can't run no more**
> **With that lawless crowd**
> **While the killers in high places**
> **Say their prayers out loud**
> **… they've summoned up**
> **A thundercloud**
> **And they're going to hear from me.**

This verse is a comment on the state of the world, on the corruption of governments and on unscrupulous corporations. The lawless crowd behave with impunity, doing whatever they wish, while the killers in high places pray aloud. They have, he says, '**summoned up a thundercloud**'. The consequence of failing to heed the signs he sings about in verse three have led, first to dysfunctional government and ultimately, in verse four, to injustice, violence and disaster.

But there may be more to the '**lawless crowd**' than just a bunch of unrestrained people behaving illegally. In Cohen's terminology, to be lawless can imply the refusal to accept the validity of the Law – the Law he sang about in the song of the same name on his *Various Positions* album. He made this point explicitly in his *Book of Mercy*, his collection of psalm-like poems, in which he condemned Israel and all nations of breaking the covenant with Mercy. 'Therefore ... the Law will never serve the lawless.' The Law, or Covenant, is the Torah; the lawless are those who will not conform to its demands for Mercy; those who take their cues from '**the killers in high places**'.[28]

The '**high places**' are the idolatrous altars condemned in the Hebrew Bible. 'I will destroy your high places, and cut down your sun-pillars, and cast your carcasses upon the carcasses of your idols; and My soul shall abhor you', rages Leviticus. The books of the prophets describe acts of shocking cruelty carried out on these altars. The killers in these high places are not common murderers and criminals; they are the idolatrous priests, evangelists of an alien, despised morality. The prophet Jeremiah blamed Israel's exile on those who committed abominations on the 'high places': those killers who sacrificed their children to the idol Baal.[29]

There are consequences, Cohen tells us, to rejecting the Law and committing murderous abominations on idolatrous altars: '**They've summoned up a thundercloud**.'

The prophet Samuel summoned up a thundercloud as a rebuke to the Israelites, after they had demanded that he appoint a king for them. In a critique almost as relevant today as it was nearly 3,000 years ago, Samuel warned the people that having a monarch is not a good thing. The king will tax them, requisition their land, conscript their children and generally make their lives a misery. God is their king, Samuel told them. By seeking a human ruler they were spurning God. But the people insisted on having a king, and Samuel reluctantly anointed Saul as the first Israelite monarch.

But Samuel did not let the matter rest there. He warned both the people and the king always to obey God's word or face retribution. He gave them a sign to drive his message home. Even though it was the height of summer, in a Middle Eastern climate where the skies are clear from early spring to late autumn, he summoned up a thundercloud. The skies poured with rain.

Cohen's message is clear. When a nation and its government fail to abide by the ethical principles of a God-fearing society, when the crowd is lawless and the killers in high places arrogantly pray out loud, the thundercloud of retribution will be summoned. It is then, says Cohen, typically introducing a flourish of humour at the culmination of his theme, that they will hear from him.

For his final descent into the well of tradition, Cohen returns to the mystical symbolism of the Kabbalah. '**You can add up the parts, but you won't have the sum**.' This is an allusion to the kabbalistic notion of God as inexpressible infinity, beyond all thought and imagination. In kabbalistic symbolism, God acts on the world through a chain of mystical powers, the Tree of Life that Cohen alluded to in *You Know Who I Am*. The material world is at the base of the tree; God's crown is at the top. Between them are the powers. Known as *sefirot*, they are the building blocks of the cosmos. But God himself is beyond all this. Known as *ein sof* ('without end'), he transcends and exceeds all the parts. Even when they are added together, the parts can never produce the sum. For although one may be able to draw closer, infinity can never be realized.

I think it is one of the best songs I have written, maybe the best. It's up there with 'If It Be Your Will' and 'Take This Waltz.' It is saying there is a crack in everything – forget about your perfect offering. I knew that song was everything that my whole work and life had somehow gathered around. It is absolutely true to me.[30]

INTERLUDE: LEONARD COHEN'S ARTWORK

Anthem is a testament to Leonard Cohen's ability to use words to paint images. But words were not his only descriptive tool.

Cohen is famous for his music, his poetry and his novels. Far less well known is that he was a prolific and talented artist. His line drawings appear on several of his album covers and in his publications, most notably in his 2006 collection of poetry *Book of Longing*, where they appear on nearly every page. One of his most striking yet simple images is the one of two interlocking hearts that he designed for the cover of the *Book of Mercy*. It looks like a star of David, but in place of triangles there are pointed hearts. Cohen called it 'the Order of the Unified Heart'.

Cohen drew nearly every day. It was a private activity, unstructured and not connected with his work. When his children were small, there would be crayons and paper on the table perpetually; drawing was just one of the things that went on in the Cohen household, without fuss and without ceremony. There was a time, he once said, when he would sketch a self-portrait when he got up every morning 'just as a way to start the day'.[31] Most of his drawings are simple line sketches, and his self-portraits, which tend to show him looking glum or puzzled, are often accompanied by a brief explanatory caption.

Much of the artwork in *Book of Longing* was drawn when Cohen was living in the monastery on Mount Baldy. The drawings include sketches of his teacher Roshi, of his old

friend Irving Layton and of Pierre Trudeau, the former
Canadian Prime Minister, a long-standing acquaintance of
Cohen's. There are also many naked or semi-naked women
and lots of self-portraits. For a long time he thought he had
lost most of his artwork; he had stored his pictures in the
offices of his former manager, who had taken them home
after she was accused of embezzling his money. He only got
them back when his lawyers obtained a Writ of Possession.

To mark the publication of *Book of Longing* the composer
Philip Glass constructed a song cycle based on Cohen's poems
and images. Cohen provided the artwork, to use as a backdrop
to the stage. The song cycle was premièred in Toronto on 1
June 2007. Two days later an exhibition of Cohen's art, entitled
Drawn in Words, opened in the city's Drabinsky Gallery. It was
the exhibition's première; from Toronto it would travel around
the world, notably to Richard Goodall's gallery in Manchester.
Goodall, Cohen said, had been asking him for years to exhibit
his work, but he had never taken the suggestion seriously; he
had always seen his art as a personal activity and had never
thought about it as a professional enterprise. Nevertheless
the exhibition was surprisingly well stocked, with dozens
of sketches, including his trademark self-portraits and
iconography. On one wall were several large images that dated
back over 20 or 30 years. They were a departure from Cohen's
usual compositions, and he admitted that he had photoshopped
some of the older pictures to 'make them better'.

Some years earlier Cohen had dismissed the idea of ever
earning money from his art. 'The great pleasure of drawing

and painting for me is that it has absolutely no professional application. It's not at all connected with anything. So I do it freely, and with a great deal of pleasure.'[32] But his financial situation had changed; he had lost his money, and the exhibition was a financial priority. It was successful. The sales helped him to recoup some of the money that had been stolen and gave him a cushion, removing the urgency of once again going on tour. Nevertheless, he still considered his art as an extracurricular activity. 'I never meant to be an artist. Or the other things.'[33]

THE WINDOW
Recent Songs (1979)

Leonard Cohen's 1979 recording *The Window* is packed with kabbalistic imagery and ideas. It is based partly on the concept of the mystical ascent of the soul; but, as we should expect, since few of Leonard Cohen's songs are straightforward, it is more than just a manual on how to meditate one's soul into heaven.

The ascent of the soul is a theme that has fascinated and perplexed philosophers and esoteric thinkers of all traditions at least from Plato onwards. In occult thought a soul can visit heaven without the body dying; with enough practice and preparation a suitably adept mystic can leave the body behind, ascend on high and return refreshed and invigorated.

As is generally the case in Cohen's music, it is his use of language rather than the song's theme that dominates. *The Window* is no different: absorbed by his lyrics we can lose sight of the theme of the song completely. He had an unmatched ability to articulate over-used, pedestrian phrases like 'body and spirit' in ear-catching new ways: 'a tangle of matter and ghost'.

The Window was recorded on the *Recent Songs* album. It was far from the best time in Cohen's life. He was deeply upset by the recent breakdown of his relationship with Suzanne and its impact on his children. And he was still getting over the trauma of recording the album *Death of a Ladies' Man* with Phil Spector. Spector's style of record production had been very different from anything that Cohen had ever experienced, and the atmosphere that he chose to work in was dark and violent. Cohen later described it as dangerous; he was terrified that one of the guns that Spector kept in the studio might go off.

> One time he came over to me about four in the morning with half a bottle of Manischewitz [sickly sweet red wine] in one hand and a .45 in the other and he put his arm around my shoulder and shoved the nozzle of the .45 into my neck and cocked it and said 'I love you, Cohen.'[34]

Cohen mentions windows dozens of times in his work, in his songs, poetry and prose. Sometimes they are conventional windows, through which he sees things, or at which people appear. But some of his windows open up on to deeper mysteries.

> **Why do you stand by the window**
> **Abandoned to beauty and pride**
> **The thorn of the night in your bosom**
> **The spear of the age in your side?**

A window, of course is where the light gets in. In the book of poetry *Death of a Lady's Man*, which he published shortly after the similarly named album he recorded with Spector, he wrote of windows and apertures that attract light or desire. In the early song *So Long, Marianne* he calls his lover to the window so that he can read her palm. Windows for Cohen can symbolize the porous boundary between two states, through which light, desire or some other ethereal quality is able to pass.

The window that has given this song its name is the boundary between body and soul, between the earthly and the divine. The person who Cohen is singing to is standing at this boundary. He challenges them. Why stand there? Why not pass through? It is obvious to him that, by standing there, they continue to suffer, their body wounded by the 'thorn of the night' and the 'spear of the age'.

He tells them he can see their distress. It is as if they are being crucified, pierced by the darkness of night and the trials of the age. Frailly human, susceptible to both beauty and pride, the suffering body, we are told in the second part of the verse, has become lost to fragrance, sickness and remorse. Its nerves are jangling.

The adversities of life have pierced this body sensually and emotionally; they've damaged its physical and emotional well-being. The body is troubled and the soul is tormented. But it can be healed.

Oh chosen love, Oh frozen love
Oh tangle of matter and ghost … Gentle this soul.

The healing will come about through love, as the chorus makes clear. Love acting on flesh and spirit, on matter and ghost. '**Tangle of matter and ghost**' is one of Leonard Cohen's most evocative epigrams, depicting as it does the interdependency of body and mind. The use of the word 'ghost' for 'spirit' has an ancient pedigree: the Holy Ghost in Christianity and the Holy Spirit in Judaism are one and the same thing.

Flesh and spirit, matter and ghost are enmeshed within us; soon Cohen will begin to describe how he believes they interrelate. But first he turns to theology, blending Christian and Jewish mystical symbols as he does so.

> **And come forth from the cloud of unknowing**
> **And kiss the cheek of the moon**
> **The New Jerusalem glowing ...**

The Cloud of Unknowing is the title of an anonymous, mystical fourteenth-century Christian text. Cohen, who read widely and took a profound interest in matters of the soul, would undoubtedly have heard of this book, perhaps even read it. *The Cloud of Unknowing* discusses a method of contemplative introspection, in which the mind divests itself of all thought and image. Properly performed and accomplished in a spirit of love, this unknowing, clouded mind is mystically conducted to a union with the divine, the very purpose that Cohen is encouraging in whoever he is singing to.

Passing through the boundary of the window, ascending heavenward, the soul will kiss the cheek of the moon. In Kabbalah, the moon is an epithet for the divine presence, the *Shechinah,* the aspect of God that manifests itself on earth, that those of us who are spiritually attuned may be able to sense or even encounter. In kissing '**the cheek of the moon**', the soul will draw closer to the divine. As it draws close, it will be granted a vision of the 'New Jerusalem'.

'New Jerusalem' is mentioned in several books written during what is known as the inter-testamental period, after the Hebrew Bible was completed and before the books of the New Testament were composed. It appears most famously in the book of Revelation, the mysterious, ominous, apocalyptic text with which the New Testament concludes.

In his song *By the Rivers Dark* Cohen used Revelation's description of Babylon as the 'great mother of earth's abominations' to symbolize sin and corruption. In contrast, 'New Jerusalem' is everything that Babylon is not. It is the city of God that will descend from heaven at the end of time, the bride of Christ, the place where there will be no death, the dwelling place of the *Shechinah*, of the moon whose cheek the soul has kissed.

Having shown the soul what it can accomplish through mystical union, if only it would pass through the window, Cohen challenges it further in the second part of the verse. He asks why it chooses to tarry in the ruin all night. The ruins may allude to the old Jerusalem, the Jerusalem of history, the destroyed city and temple that Jewish prayers yearn to rebuild. Elliot Wolfson, professor of Jewish mysticism, believes so. In his scholarly analysis of *The Window* he notes that in the version of the song that Cohen published in his collection *Stranger Music: Selected Poems and Songs* the reference to 'New Jerusalem' was deleted. Wolfson wonders whether Cohen had second thoughts about the implications of juxtaposing 'New Jerusalem' with a comment about people tarrying in the ruin. Since 'New Jerusalem' symbolizes the Christian messianic future, Cohen may have worried that tarrying in the ruin might be understood as a negative stereotype of Jews, remaining stubbornly in the old Jerusalem even though 'New Jerusalem' was already available.[35]

As the second verse draws to a close, Cohen explains to the soul what it must do if it is to arise from its despair, to ascend from the piercing of its body. Rather than tarrying in the ruin, he tells the soul, it should

> **Climb upon your tears and be silent**
> **Like a rose on its ladder of thorns.**

The Zohar, the thirteenth-century, Spanish-Jewish compilation of legend, fable and mystical theology that became the principal text of Kabbalah, tells us about the rose. It quotes a verse from the Song of Songs: 'as a rose among the thorns, so is my beloved among the daughters'. The rose, says the Zohar, is a metaphor for Israel or, as Cohen chooses to understand it, the soul. Just as a rose can be red or white, symbolizing Justice and Mercy respectively, so the soul is susceptible to each of these powers. The thorns that surround the rose symbolize the severities of judgement; the flower's petals stand for mercy. Cohen urges the soul to silently rise above the thorns. When this happens, the Zohar says, the thorns will wither and drop off, leaving the rose pristine in its purity, surrounded by the petals of Mercy.[36]

Roses and thorns also occur in the work of the medieval Persian poet Rumi, who, Cohen acknowledged, had a significant impact on his work. He indicated that *The Window* was one of the songs influenced by Rumi. The Sufi poet Rumi lived at the same time as the Zohar was being composed, and there are recognized correspondences between Sufism and Kabbalah. It is of little surprise that the symbolism in *The Window* evokes both Rumi's work and the Kabbalah. Cohen's music and poetry are invariably capable of being viewed through more than one lens.[37]

> **Then lay your rose on the fire**
> **The fire give up to the sun**
> **The sun give over to splendour**
> **In the arms of the High Holy One.**

The imagery is tantalizing. The rose is now consumed by an ever-increasing light – light, presumably, that comes through the window. As it is consumed, the rose ascends, until it reaches the High Holy One, its mystical union with the divine. This, Cohen is telling the soul, is what it is capable of achieving. If only it would stop standing by the window, abandoned to the fleshly cravings for beauty and the pitfalls of pride.

We could imagine the song ending there. But, as we might expect, it does not. For, just as we think we have the measure of what he is singing about, Leonard Cohen often manages to push us just a little further. There is a further idea he wants to introduce.

> **For the holy one dreams of a letter**
> **Dreams of a letter's death**
> **Oh bless thee continuous stutter**
> **Of the word being made into flesh.**

Cohen spoke briefly about *The Window* in a 1979 concert in a Munich TV studio. He said: 'it's a kind of prayer, to bring the two parts of the soul together.' The idea that the soul is comprised of various parts goes back to ancient Greek philosophy. Aristotle divided the soul into two parts – the rational and the irrational – and then subdivided each part further.

The idea of a composite soul developed over the centuries; different philosophical schools had varying views about what the parts of the soul were and how they related to each other. Jewish mysticism was influenced by Neoplatonism, and by a view that the soul was divided into a heavenly and an earthly part. This idea became important in the mystical branch of Hasidism known as Habad. The eighteenth-century founder of Habad, Schneur Zalman of Liady, wrote about the tension between our animal and heavenly souls, between our instinct for physical survival and our desire for something beyond the physical confines of this world.

In an interview with the Jewish writer and scholar Arthur Kurzweil, Cohen mentioned his conversations about Judaism with Rabbi Simcha Zirkind, who ran the Habad mission at

McGill University, where Cohen studied. It may have been these conversations that started Cohen thinking about the process of reconciling the two parts of the soul, about bringing them together.

In the first part of this final verse he sang about the ascent of the soul into the 'arms of the High Holy One'. Now we see movement in the opposite direction, the Holy One dreaming of the Word turning into flesh.

The Gospel of John explains about the Word becoming flesh. 'In the beginning was the Word and the word was with God.' In the original Greek of the New Testament the Word is called *logos,* it's where we get our word 'logic' from. The Word, or *logos*, is divine reason, the ultimate cause of everything, that which existed within God before the cosmos came into being. 'The Word', the Gospel continues, 'became flesh and lives amongst us and we have seen his glory, the glory as of a father's only son.' The Word became incarnate as Christ. It is this idea of incarnation that Cohen had in mind when he sang that the Holy One dreams of the 'word being made into flesh'.

Habad philosophy talks about reconciling the two parts of the soul within each of us. Cohen seems to see the process of reconciliation more dynamically. As the soul ascends mystically heavenward, the Word descends into our flesh. Our flesh and the animal soul within it are transformed; uniting with the heavenly soul, the two souls are now one. But the transformation is not a single event; it is an ongoing process, the soul arising, the Word descending, in a '**continuous stutter**'.

For Cohen the Word becoming flesh is not a unique process, as it is in conventional Christian theology, accomplished through the incarnation of Christ. Rather, he sees it as an ongoing dynamic: initiated by the desire of our soul to ascend, causing a corresponding descent from above. The two parts of the soul, the human and the divine, reaching out in a state of creative tension towards each other, joining together interweaving, communing as one. The transformation of the earthly soul into a divine being. '**Oh tangle of matter and ghost … Gentle this soul**.'

YOU HAVE LOVED ENOUGH
Ten New Songs (2001)

> **I said I'd be your lover**
> **You laughed at what I said**
> **I lost my job forever**
> **I was counted with the dead**

Sometimes when we listen to a Leonard Cohen song we hear words that sound so simple and straightforward that we fail to discern any deeper meaning in them. We may realize they have a deeper meaning only when we hear a subsequent verse, and realize that the whole song is based on an idea we hadn't spotted.

The short song *You Have Loved Enough* is one such example. It was recorded in 2001, on *Ten New Songs*, Cohen's first album for nine years. *Ten New Songs* was a collaboration with Sharon Robinson, his long-term songwriting partner, accompanying vocalist and friend. They had been recording and performing together for over 20 years, Cohen was the godfather to her son. The album, he said 'could be described as a duet'.[38]

On the face of it, *You have Loved Enough* seems to be a love song, in which the singer is being kept at a distance by the lover he desires. But Cohen had said that the song was based on a poem of the same name, a poem which in 1999 he made publicly available on the Leonard Cohen Files website. In the website version of the poem, every time he addresses the lover, he writes 'You', with a capital Y. The final line, in which the lover finally speaks, reads '**now let Me be the Lover**'. The deliberate changes of case suggest that the poem is a conversation, not with another person, but with God, whose name Cohen always wrote as G-d, and to whose pronouns he always gave a capital letter.[39]

> **I swept the marble chambers**
> **But You sent me down below**
> **You kept me from believing**
> **Until you let me know.**

It is the '**marble chambers**' that lead us to realize that *You Have Loved Enough* is more than a love song.

The early Jewish mystical tradition tells a story of four rabbis who undertook an excursion to a place called the *pardes*. *Pardes* is a Persian word for 'garden'; it is the origin of our word 'paradise'. The story is about a mystical journey that the four rabbis made to the heavenly realms.

The leader of the expedition was a man named Rabbi Akiva. He was a prophet of love; it was due to Akiva's advocacy that the erotic poem Song of Songs was included in the Bible. He saw it as a parable of the love between God and humanity. 'All books of the Bible are holy,' he said, 'but Song of Songs is the holiest of the holy.'[40]

Akiva was an experienced mystic; he had made the journey to heaven before. He warned his three, less experienced companions: 'when you arrive at the stones of pure marble do not cry "water, water".' The marble in the chambers through which they would pass was so pure and translucent, he warned them, that they might mistake it for water.[41] But they were not to declare that it was water. One may not misspeak in heaven.

The expedition was not a success. The journey was fraught with danger, and only Akiva returned unscathed. One of his companions died: he is the one whom Cohen refers to as being sent down below. Another abandoned his faith, becoming a heretic: as Cohen puts it, '**You kept me from believing**'. And the third, a young man named Ben Zoma, went mad.

These events help explain the first verse. The rabbi who became a heretic lost his job for ever, the one who went mad was laughed at, and the one who died was '**counted with the dead**'. They had all followed Akiva's example of proclaiming their love for God, saying, '**I'd be your lover**'.

Ben Zoma, the heavenly voyager who went mad, was a moderate man. He is quoted in the Talmud as saying, 'Who is rich? He who is happy with what he has. Who is strong? He who controls his passions.' But he also declared that he had been surveying the gap between the waters of heaven and those of earth, and had discovered that the space was no more than three fingers wide. This prompted one of his teachers to suggest that his mind was still disturbed. 'Ben Zoma,' he said, 'is still outside.'[42]

I am not the one who loves
It's love that seizes me ...

Ben Zoma went mad because the intensity of the revelation he experienced was too much for him to bear. Seized by love, drowning in heavenly bliss, he was overwhelmed.

And when the hunger for Your touch,
Rises from the hunger …

Ben Zoma's hunger is no ordinary hunger. His hunger is compounded, his rapacity for the divine touch arising out of the yearning he already feels, the hunger of his love. His was a hunger that cannot be satiated, an eternal, blissful craving.

The rabbis of the Talmud explained what had happened to Ben Zoma by quoting a verse from the book of Proverbs: 'Have you found honey? Eat no more than your fill, lest you overeat and become sick.'[43] Ben Zoma found honey, the nectar of heavenly ecstasy. He could not satisfy his craving; he overate and became sick, losing his mind.

But all is not lost for Ben Zoma. Cohen lets us hear God's voice, the voice of healing, reassuring Ben Zoma that his love was not unrequited.

You have loved enough,
Now let me be the Lover.

And now we realize why Cohen gave the song the title that it has.

5

PRAYER

When Bob Dylan heard Cohen's 1984 album *Various Positions*, he said his songs were becoming almost like prayers. He was using the word 'prayer' loosely: conventional prayers are petitions, formally written and often using words that sound archaic in ordinary speech. Cohen's prayers are more like conversations, with someone who may be God – however he conceived him to be – but who might equally be a lover. They are prayers for renewal, for return, for healing. Sometimes we only hear Cohen's side of the conversation. As with most prayers, we don't get to hear a reply.

Cohen learned about prayer as a child in the synagogue. Many of the prayers he heard were lengthy and wordy, written in Hebrew, a language of which most congregants had only a basic grasp. The idea behind Jewish prayer is that their recitation helps to concentrate the mind and elevate the spirit. In practice, however, their sheer length and impenetrability can make them feel stultifying and opaque. When Cohen wrote prayers based on those he had heard as a child, it was because he had the knowledge to reach behind the fog of words to extract an idea or phrase that resonated.

There are many different types of prayer in the Bible. Some, like Jacob's petition after his dream of the ladder to heaven, humbly invoke God's protection. Others, such as Abraham's attempt to save Sodom from destruction, or Moses' entreaties on behalf of the Israelites, are more confrontational, trying to reason with God instead of begging him. None of these prayers made it into later Christian or Jewish liturgy. The Priestly Blessing from the book of Numbers did. So did the Lord's Prayer, which, echoing the development of prayers in the ancient synagogue, conformed to a new protocol of first praising God before making a request.

But of all the biblical prayers that are in use in church and synagogue today, the vast majority come from the book of Psalms, poems that combine awe of God with a sense of wonder at the created world. It was the book of Psalms that inspired *Book of Mercy*, which Cohen composed in the early 1980s, at a time when he was renewing his connection to Judaism.

Book of Mercy, a collection of 50 odes, was published in the same year as the *Various Positions* album. Described by its publisher as Leonard Cohen's 'classic book of contemporary psalms', the book is replete with reworkings of Jewish themes: prayers, Talmudic legends, kabbalistic meditations and philosophical debates. In an interview with the late poet Robert Sward, Cohen described it as 'a secret book … a sacred kind of conversation'.

Cohen called *Book of Mercy* 'an important document', but said that it was 'a little book of prayer that is only valuable to someone who needs it at the time'. There are no poems from *Book of Mercy* on the *Various Positions* album. They are too personal. The prayers on *Various Positions* have a more universal application; they are prayers for sharing with his audience. 'A popular song,' Cohen said, 'has to move more easily, lip to lip.'[1]

Cohen's prayers rarely address specific social or political issues. Only once does he acknowledge that he is praying for some sort of worldly change. In *The Land of Plenty*, a protest song in which he questions whether he even has the right to protest, and never quite makes it clear which injustice he is protesting about, he tells us:

> I lift my voice and pray.
> May the lights in The Land of Plenty
> Shine on the truth some day.

WHO BY FIRE
New Skin for the Old Ceremony (1974)

> **And who by fire, who by water ...**
> **... who in your merry, merry month of May,**
> **Who by very slow decay,**
> **And who shall I say is calling?**

Some time early in the second century CE, Rabbi Ishmael son of Elisha separated himself from his wife and entered a dark room. He remained there for 40 days, drinking only a little water at night. Every half-hour, 48 times each day, he would immerse himself in a ritual bath, from the soles of his feet to the crown of his head. When he wasn't immersing, he recited prayers and chanted incantations. He did not sleep.

Towards the end of the 40th day his students entered the room and sat in a circle around him. Ishmael, by now very weak, bent forward and placed his head between his knees. As his body went limp, his soul embarked on a mystical journey to the Palace of the Seventh Heaven. If his preparations had been correct and his soul pure, he knew the angels would gather him up. They would place him on the right hand side of the Chariot, the very Throne of God, described in the opening words of the prophet Ezekiel's book. Alongside the Chariot he would be shown all that was destined to happen in the world. Back on earth his students would be watching his prone body anxiously, ready to bring him back should it appear that anything was going wrong.

As he ascended, Ishmael chanted these words:

Who shall be cast down, who exalted;
Who shall be weakened, who made strong;
Who shall be crushed with poverty, who made rich;
Who shall die, who shall live;
From whom shall inheritance be taken,
To whom shall inheritance be given;
Who shall be granted the Law for his portion
And who be given Wisdom.[2]

The chant is recorded in a mystical tract known as *Hechalot Rabbati*, or the *Great Palaces*. The date of the tract is not known; scholarly opinions range between the second and sixth centuries CE.

In the eleventh century, according to another legend, Rabbi Amnon of the German city of Mainz came under intense pressure from the city's archbishop to convert to Christianity. But no matter how often or how aggressively he was urged, time and again Amnon refused, until one day it all became too much for him. He felt unable to hold out any longer, and asked the archbishop for three days' grace to consider the demand. The archbishop agreed, and Amnon set off for home.

As soon as he left the archbishop's palace Rabbi Amnon was overcome by regret. He wished he had not made such a foolish request. He knew he could never abandon his faith, his people or his God.

When the third day dawned, Amnon did not return to the palace. The archbishop sent his soldiers to seize him. As he was led into the archbishop's presence, Amnon cried out that he had been a fool; his request for three days' grace had been unworthy. His tongue, he advised, should be cut out. But the archbishop did not blame Amnon's tongue. He blamed his feet, for not bringing him back sooner. He ordered that Amnon's hands and feet be cut off.

Amnon's body was mutilated on the first day of the Jewish New Year, a day when all his congregation were present in the synagogue. Bleeding profusely and dying, Amnon's final wish was that he be brought to them. As he was being carried into the Mainz synagogue, a lengthy hymn, a composition never previously heard, poured from his lips. Some of it sounded a little like the incantation that Ishmael son of Elisha had recited nearly a thousand years earlier. He concluded with the following words:

Who will live and who will die;
Who in his due time and who not in his due time;
Who by water and who by fire,
Who by the sword and who by beasts,
Who by famine and who by thirst,
Who by earthquake and who by plague,
Who by strangling and who by stoning.
Who will rest and who will wander,

Who will be tranquil and who will be harassed,
Who will be at ease and who will be troubled,
Who will be rich and who will be poor,
Who will be brought down and who will be raised up?
But Repentance, Prayer and Charity avert the severe
　　decree.

Amnon was a historical character, and although the legend is almost certainly not true, the poem dates from at least his time, if not earlier. A handwritten copy was found in the Cairo Genizah, an ancient repository of Hebrew texts discovered at the end of the nineteenth century.

Over a thousand years before Rabbi Amnon was said to have composed this poem, and several hundred before Ishmael's heaven-bound song was recited, a cuneiform tablet was engraved in Babylon. The tablet seems to be an instruction manual for astrologers; it shows them how to read a horoscope. Among the fates that can be divined are life and death, wealth and poverty, death by sword and death at one's ordained time. One scholar suggests that there is a connection between the Babylonian tablet and the poem allegedly written by Rabbi Amnon.[3]

So, Amnon's eleventh-century poem has its roots in a Babylonian astrological manual dating from the second century BCE, and an incantation recited by heavenly voyagers several hundred years before Amnon lived. It has come down to us as part of the synagogue liturgy, recited on New Year and the Day of Atonement, days that lend themselves to reflection and personal introspection. Its stark message and the simplicity of its language and metre have led it to become one of the musical highlights of the Jewish liturgical calendar, sung in contemporary congregations to rousing arrangements. It is little wonder that the prayer stuck in Leonard Cohen's mind when he first heard it, in synagogue with his uncles at the age of five. *Who by Fire*, his reworking of the composition attributed to Rabbi Amnon, was first released in 1974 on his album *New Skin for the Old Ceremony*. He sang it as a duet with Janis Ian.

Cohen spoke about *Who by Fire* in a 1979 interview, explaining about the Book of Life, which in Jewish tradition lies open in heaven between the New Year and the Day of Atonement. During these ten days, the names of all are inscribed, along with their fate for the coming year, whether they will live or whether they will die. The prayer, said Cohen, is a catalogue of all the various ways in which one can quit 'this vale of tears'. The melody in *Who by Fire*, 'if not actually stolen, is certainly derived from the melody that I heard in the synagogue as a boy'.[4]

As we might expect, Cohen approached the prayer from his own perspective. The synagogue version is, as he said, a catalogue, a matter-of-fact list of the type of life we might expect to lead over the coming year or, if we are unfortunate, the ways in which we might meet our end. Some of the deaths are natural; others are accidental. A couple are the result of decrees by earthly courts: stoning and strangling are, according to the Talmud, two of the four capital penalties mandated by the Bible.[5] The remaining verses offer examples of the types of lives that those who survive the year might, or might not, enjoy.

Cohen's catalogue, in his unique style, manages to be both dark and playful. He has people dying from barbiturates, by their own hand and in solitude; others meet their end in the '**merry, merry month of May**', by their '**lady's command**' or in '**realms of love**'. It is not apparent whether he has specific people in mind, but it would be odd if he wasn't thinking of a few former friends or acquaintances as he composed his lyric.

But it is the end of *Who by Fire* that should grab our attention; it is this rather than the list of unhappy demises which differentiates Cohen's song from its medieval forerunner. The medieval prayer is one of submissive piety; its dooms may have been terrifying to a medieval supplicant, but at least it offered them a remedy. The final line acknowledges that their destiny can be changed, even once it has been ordained. All that is required is sufficient piety: Repentance, Prayer and Charity. The fateful decree can be overturned if one is willing to heed the call.

Cohen is not so pliant. He does not seem concerned with whether or how the decree may be changed. Rather than heeding the call to repentance, the more important matter for him is the final line in each of the three verses: '**Who shall I say is calling?**' It is not, as some have suggested, a query asked by a telephone receptionist. It is an existential question that bothers him.

Cohen's question is anticipated by the opening passage of the original prayer, a section that he did not incorporate into the song, which precedes the catalogue of possible fates. The passage describes the heavenly court sitting in judgement on the Day of Atonement, with God opening the Book of Remembrances and inscribing their fate within it. The great *shofar*, the heavenly trumpet, is sounded, a thin, silent voice is heard and the angels are seized by fear and trembling.

It is the thin, silent voice that answers Cohen's question 'Who shall I say is calling?' Translated in the King James Bible as 'a still, small voice', it was heard by the prophet Elijah when he was fleeing from Queen Jezebel, who had vowed to kill him. As he stood on the mountain awaiting God's word, a terrifying, rock-shattering wind passed before him. Elijah waited, expecting to hear God's voice thundering from the tempest. But God is not in the wind. An earthquake shook his mountain. Again he waited, but God was not in the earthquake. Then a fire, but God was not in that either. Finally, he hears a 'still, small voice', a 'thin, silent voice'. That is the voice of God.[6]

It is the thin, silent voice of God, calling and agitating the angels in the opening verses of the prayer, that Cohen is asking about. He is asking because, as someone intimately familiar with the Bible, he knows that Elijah, the only person to hear the still small voice, is also the only biblical character not to die. Instead, Elijah is seen by his disciple Elisha to ascend to heaven, borne aloft into a whirlwind by a chariot of fire, drawn by fiery horses.[7]

This is the conundrum. The still, small voice determining who will live and die, the voice heard only by the one who did not die, the voice which calls the departing soul to heaven. Whose is this voice, asks Cohen. Who is calling?

Cohen summed it up in a conversation with the film-maker Harry Rasky. 'Who is calling? That is what makes the song into a prayer, for me in my terms: who is it, or what is it that determines who will live and who will die? What is the source of this great furnace of creation? Who lights it? Who extinguishes it?'[8] Prayer for Cohen, at least in *Who by Fire*, is neither a petition nor a route map to a new destiny. It is a quest for Truth.

COMING BACK TO YOU
Various Positions (1984)

The Country-and-Western-inspired love song *Coming Back to You* records the struggle of someone trying to return to an unreliable, perhaps an unfaithful, lover. It was recorded on the *Various Positions* album, often said to be the most religiously inspired of all of Cohen's records, where *Hallelujah*, *If It Be Your Will* and *The Law* are also to be found.

The album *Various Positions* was released in 1984, the year that Cohen turned 50. It was a time when he began looking more deeply into his Judaism, integrating it more fully into his life. He was studying the Talmud, and he spiced his poetry with an intensely Jewish flavour. In October 1984 he released *Book of Mercy,* his collection of 50 psalm-like poems.

Various Positions has been described as the musical counterpoint to the *Book of Mercy.* Apart from the religiously influenced *Hallelujah* and *If It Be Your Will,* Jewish themes crop up in nearly every song. He told Arthur Kurzweil that his renewed interest in Judaism came about after he damaged his knees in a fall and could no longer practise his Zen meditations. His biographer Ira Nadel suggests that his religious renewal was partly influenced by the breakdown of his marriage to Suzanne Elrod in the late 1970s. In another song on the album, *The Night Comes On*, he sings of turning to religion while locked in a kitchen, wondering how long 'she' (presumably Suzanne) would stay.[9]

Various Positions had a difficult debut. Cohen had just discovered electronic musical technology. He'd bought himself a small, inexpensive Casio keyboard that he insisted on using on the album, even though the sound quality was not as good the expensive, new, state-of-the-art synthesizer that his producer tried to persuade him to use. But the real crisis for *Various Positions* was that his record company decided not to issue it in the United States. 'Leonard, we know you are great, we just don't know if you are any good,' they told him.[10]

Cohen was typically understanding: 'What I understand now, very thoroughly, is that the dollar they spend on promoting me can much more profitably be spent on promoting another singer, so I have no quarrel with it. I don't think I suffered any sense of remorse or bitterness.'[11]

Various Positions was released elsewhere in the world, but it didn't fare very well. The only countries where it enjoyed any measure of success were Norway and Sweden. It reached number 52 in the UK charts. But in time the album would be more than vindicated. *Hallelujah* is one of the most recorded songs of all time, and *Dance Me to the End of Love* is among his most popular tracks. These days *Various Positions* is considered a classic.

Cohen may not have been bitter that the album was not released in the USA, but its failure to have an impact was a setback. His career had not been going well. He was short of money, and was feeling creatively stymied. For the past few years he had been living peripatetically, keeping a low public profile, shuttling from one home to another. He still had his flat in Montreal and the house he had purchased on the Greek island of Hydra. When he wasn't in either of those places he was at the Buddhist monastery on Mount Baldy, or flying to Provence, to the farmhouse in Bonnieux which he had bought for Suzanne and their two children, Adam and Lorca. When he was there, he would stay in a trailer in the grounds.

His sluggish career and many commitments were draining his resources, psychologically and financially. As it turned out, that insecurity may have been exactly what he needed. Never afraid to work hard, Cohen threw himself into his work, overcoming the psychological blocks that were impeding his creativity. 'When things got really desperate,' he said, 'I started to cheer up.'[12]

Cohen spoke of *Coming Back to You* as 'really the same song' as *So Long, Marianne* and *The Gypsy's Wife*, 'rooted in some kind of inspired confusion of womanhood, godliness, beauty and darkness. It was the world I lived in, and it was true.'[13] Like those songs, it treats of lost love. Unlike them, it resonates with the language of the Bible, with words from both Testaments and the liturgy of synagogue and church. *Coming Back to You* is a song both of a man returning to a lover and of a supplicant seeking to return to God. There is no qualitative difference for Cohen between the longing of the heart and the longing of the soul.

Religiously, Cohen hung *Coming Back to You* on the same peg as *Who by Fire* – on the theme of repentance and judgement that dominates the autumnal synagogue liturgy and occupies the mind of the religious Jew in the days between the New Year and Yom Kippur, the Day of Atonement. Emotionally, it is the confession of a lover who regrets the past and knows he has to work at getting the relationship right. The only difference between the religious and emotional aspects of the song is who, or what, he is addressing.

> **Maybe I'm still hurting,**
> **I can't turn the other cheek,**
> **But you know that I still love you,**
> **It's just that I can't speak.**

Cohen knows that, whether one is trying to return to God or to a lover, humility is a necessary condition for sincere repentance. So he begins by affirming the most famous exhortation to humility, the exhortation in the speech that Jesus delivers to his followers from a mountain, a speech that is so much more than a sermon but which is known as the Sermon on the Mount.

Jesus told his followers, 'If anyone slaps you on the right cheek, turn to them the other cheek also.'[14] Cohen immediately finds himself frustrated. He can't do it. He is not ready either to be shamed by the lover he is desperate to return to or to accept the chastisements he may deserve from his God. '**Maybe I'm still hurting, I can't turn the other cheek**.' Cohen's desire to return seems stymied from the very outset.

Unable to abase himself by turning the other cheek, Cohen adopts a different strategy, one that may achieve the same result in a less challenging and demanding way. He knew, from the years he spent in the synagogue while growing up, that the sabbath before the Day of Atonement is called the 'Sabbath of Return'. It was given this name because a passage is read from the prophet Hosea that encourages those who have abandoned God to return, and shows them how to do it.

Hosea begins his rallying cry, declaring: 'Return, O Israel, to the Lord your God, for you have stumbled in your sin. Take words with you and return to the Lord.'[15] Return, the prophet implies, doesn't have to involve public humiliation; words will do. Make a verbal acknowledgement of what has gone wrong and what needs to be put right. Confession, as every religion knows, is spiritual therapy.

But Cohen, who desperately wants to return, doesn't find Hosea's instruction any easier than the exhortation in the Sermon on the Mount. '**You know that I still love you, It's just that I can't speak**.' He doesn't have the words. He can't confess, he cannot speak.

Worse still, his path is strewn with obstacles. He can't pay the bills and he has no food. The factory, he sings, is closing down, and the fields have been placed under lock and key. He turns again to Hosea, who is expressing the benefits of repentance, using a pastoral metaphor: 'I will be like dew to Israel, he will blossom like a lily, he will spread his roots like a tree of Lebanon, His boughs shall spread, His beauty will be like the olive, His fragrance like Lebanon.'[16] This bucolic scene will unfold, Hosea says, when we heed the call to return. Cohen, who is still struggling to find the words, finds that he has a different experience. He is making some sort of progress, but it is intermittent. He follows Hosea in summoning up an image from rural life. But it is far less encouraging:

> And the fields they're under lock and key
> Tho' the rain and the sun come through
> And springtime starts but then it stops.

Unable to repent fully, Cohen knows what will happen next.

> And they're handing down my sentence now
> And I know what I must do
> Another mile of silence while I'm
> Coming back to you.

This is judgement day. If he cannot repent, if he is not willing to turn back from the path on which he has set himself, he will appear for sentence before the heavenly court, the court that he sang about in *Who by Fire*.

Strangely though, he is not afraid. It is as if his sincere desire to achieve repentance, despite his inability to humble himself and confess, has still counted in his favour. He knows what he has to do. He must walk in silence, partially following the advice of both Jesus and Hosea. After adjuring his followers to turn the other cheek, Jesus told them, 'If someone forces you to go one mile, go with him two.' Hosea says that the righteous walk in the paths of the Lord. But neither Jesus nor Hosea recommends walking in silence.[17]

The acclaimed scholar of Jewish mysticism Elliot Wolfson suggests that Cohen's submission to the judgement, his acknowledgement that he must walk in silence, appears distinctly un-Jewish. He wonders if a touch of Zen influence can be detected here, 'silently heeding the whirl of the karmic wheel in an effort to be liberated from its spin'.[18]

Cohen spent a considerable amount of time in the Zen monastery on Mount Baldy. It would be odd if his lyrics did not contain Zen influences. And it would be a mistake to interpret any of Leonard Cohen's works as influenced by only one source; almost everything he wrote is capable of multiple interpretations. There might well be a Zen influence here. But equally, silence need not be un-Jewish. "'I grew up all my life among the sages", said Shimon the son of Gamliel, "and I have found that there is nothing better for a person than silence."'[19]

> Since you are a shining light
> There's many that you'll see
> But I have to deal with envy
> When you choose the precious few
> Who've left their pride on the other side of
> Coming back to you.

It turns out that Cohen was right to be silent. For it transpires that his struggle to find a way to repent has led him to realize his error. It seems that he was looking for a relationship that was exclusive to him alone, that he was envious of the love that God bestows on those who are able to be selfless in their commitment to the divine. This verse doesn't seem to be addressed to a human lover. But it does now contain a confession. Cohen has owned up to being envious.

The envy that Cohen had to deal with is rooted on the 'other side', the place from where, in kabbalistic cosmology, evil emanates. The 'other side' is a dark domain, where God's light barely penetrates. It is a place where people should leave 'their pride'. Cohen is beginning to become reconciled to his problem. Pride, one of the seven deadly sins in Christianity, resides on the 'other side'. Only the very few who are self-willed enough to leave their pride there, not to carry it with them, are able to achieve a complete return, to achieve absolute repentance. Cohen has not reached that level yet. He is stricken with envy. It is his envy of those who have been able to renounce their pride which holds him back.

As he concludes his song he turns to his lover again. Cohen has made a partial return, but he still has further to go. He knows that, even in the arms of his lover,

I'll never get it right.
Even when you bend to give me
Comfort in the night.

He craves reassurance; he has to have her word that he has been accepted. If he is not, his prayer has been in vain,

Or none of it is true,
And all I've said was just instead of
Coming back to you.

LOVER, LOVER, LOVER
New Skin for the Old Ceremony (1974)

> **I asked my father, I said,**
> **'Father change my name.**
> **The one I'm using now it's covered up**
> **with fear and filth and cowardice and shame.'**

Cohen wrote *Lover, Lover, Lover* in 1973, while he was in Israel, entertaining the troops during the Yom Kippur War. It may be the fastest he ever wrote a song. When he sang it on tour, he introduced it as 'written in the Sinai desert for soldiers of both sides'. The first version of the song, however, began with him singing that he had seen 'his brothers' fighting in the desert. He revised the opening verse in Ethiopia, a few weeks later. He'd flown directly there from Israel; one of his biographers believes he went there to avoid the marital conflict waiting for him at home.[20]

He recorded the song a year after writing it. It appears on his 1974 album *New Skin for the Old Ceremony*, the same album as *Who by Fire*. The album sold well in Britain and Germany, but it failed to make a commercial impact anywhere else: it didn't even make the top 200 in the USA. The cover made a greater impression. Rather than displaying a portrait of himself, as his earlier albums had done, Cohen chose an illustration from a sixteenth-century alchemical treatise, the *Rosarium Philosophorum*, or *Rose*

Garden of the Philosophers. It depicts a naked, winged couple, with crowns on their heads. They are flying through the air, copulating. The image represents the sacred union, the holy act of love that unifies the cosmos by uniting the male and female principles. Love-making, for Cohen, was not merely gratuitous. It was a spiritual act of intense profundity — the sensual illusion he sings about in *Born In Chains*, which unified God's Name.

Like so much of Cohen's work, *Lover, Lover, Lover* has been interpreted from many different perspectives. The Czech scholar and poet Jiří Měsíc sees a strong Sufi influence in the song, reflecting Cohen's interest in the thirteenth-century poet Rumi. He suggests that the rhythmic refrain of the song recalls an Islamic chant, while the music evokes the ritual 'whirling' Sufi dance.[21]

The song begins with Cohen asking his father to change his name, because the one he has is covered in filth and shame. As the song progresses it becomes apparent that it is the heavenly father who is being addressed, rather than a biological parent. The religious imagery in the song can only credibly be interpreted as part of a dialogue with God.

It is unclear whether Cohen's sense of shame is due to a specific incident in his past or whether it is a consequence of his depressive outlook, but the remedy he draws on comes from the Talmud. Changing one's name, according to the Talmud, is a way of altering one's life and destiny. Discussing how one may avoid punishment from heaven for one's crimes, the late third-century teacher Rabbi Yitzhak states:

> A person's sentence is torn up on account of four types of actions. These are: Giving charity, crying out in prayer, changing one's name, and changing one's deeds for the better ... As it is written: 'As for Sarai your wife, you shall not call her name Sarai, but Sarah shall be her name ... And I will bless her, and I will also give you a son from her.'[22]

Changing our name changes our destiny. Abraham's wife, Sarai, was childless until God changed her name to Sarah. With a new name, and a new destiny, she became pregnant and gave birth.

Name-changes lead to a new future because our names are an indication of our spiritual essence. They are a window onto our soul. There is a Jewish custom of changing the name of a desperately ill person, in the hope that the Angel of Death will not be able to find them. The custom owes more to superstition than to mysticism, but that hasn't stopped it being a last resort, when all else has failed.

Of course, for those who are not desperately ill, changing their name is only effective if it is accompanied by a conscious effort to change the direction of their life. That's why the Talmudic discussion about changing one's destiny occurs as part of a treatise on repentance, of returning to God. Cohen picks up on the importance of return in the song's refrain,

when he calls on his lover, seven times, to come back to him.
The call is repeated twice.

> **He said I locked you in this body,**
> **I meant it as a kind of trial ...**
> **... to make some woman smile.**

The response doesn't seem to address Cohen's request to have
his name changed. God is speaking to Cohen's soul, treating
his body as ancillary to who he really is. For if names are
windows onto our souls, then a request to change one's name
is tantamount to a desire for a new soul. And that will never
do, for our souls are locked in our bodies as a kind of trial. We
can use our bodies, the verse continues, for good or bad, either
as a weapon, or 'to make some woman smile'. Our bodies are
instruments for our souls; they are, according to many mystical
traditions, the garments in which our souls are clothed.
Changing our name may be effective, but we shouldn't have to
resort to it; it is far preferable to use our bodies to remedy our
souls. As long as we don't let the body get the upper hand.

The soul's problem with the body, according to early Jewish
mystical thought, is that it is susceptible to the 'evil inclination'.
The soul can too easily give way to the body's desire for lust,
violence or greed. Physical passions may appear to serve no
higher purpose. But they do: the purpose of evil, according
to one perspective, is to give us the opportunity to overcome
our weaknesses, to give us the chance to elevate our souls
through strength of character. Evil subjects our souls to a test;

this is the trial that Cohen is singing about, to the soldiers in the desert. They may be required, for reasons beyond their control, to resort to violence; they may be overpowered by fear or hatred; but they should not lose sight of the soul's higher purpose. Rather than succumbing to the brutalization of war, the soul can strive to be elevated by, for example, making a lover smile. [23]

War, according to Cohen, is a necessary evil, but love, as the picture that he chose for the album's cover reminds us, is a spiritual act. The soul, which according to Kabbalah, comes from heaven to earth by way of the Garden of Eden, is pure and immaculate. The evil inclination seeks to taint it. But the evil inclination is not wholly bad: without sexual desire we would never start a family; without the physical need for warmth and shelter we would never build a house. [24] The trial for the soul locked in the body is to overcome the evil inclination, to take what is necessary from it for survival while remaining untainted. As Cohen said in an interview: 'Religion and war are obviously connected, and all of it is connected to the person who has to live through it … One of the reasons I use biblical references continually is because even though the culture has changed … the images contained in the Bible have remained.' [25]

'Then let me start again,' I cried.

But Cohen doesn't want the burden of a trial. He cries that he wants to start again, with a fair face and a calm spirit. He wants, he seems to be saying, to be given the chance to leave the battlefield, not to have to pay for whatever brought him there, not to be tested. And his protest ignites God's ire. '**I never turned aside or walked away**,' he replies in the penultimate verse; '**It was you who built the temple, it was you who covered up my face**.' Cohen's plea to have his name changed has been rejected. He cannot simply wipe out his responsibilities with a new identity. It wasn't God who walked away or turned aside, he is told pointedly. Cohen has done things that have led to his soul being put on trial. His offences, we hear, are not those of the body, not things like theft or violence. They are offences of the soul, offences of religion, offences that seem to be the result of practising religion in the wrong way. The offence, we may be astonished to hear, of building the Temple.

The Temple built by King Solomon in Jerusalem was the spiritual centre of Judaism for over a thousand years, bar a short break in the sixth century BCE when the Babylonians destroyed it. It was rebuilt then destroyed for a second time by the Romans, in the year 70 CE. Since then Jewish prayers have yearned for its rebuilding, for a return to the days of its former glory. The idea of the Temple is central to Judaism, and yet Cohen, as a proxy for Israel, is castigated for building it. He is told he has covered up God's face.

Solomon's Temple was intended to be a dwelling place for God. It's not a concept that means very much to us today: if we think of God at all, we don't think of him as dwelling anywhere. But in ancient times every god, of every nation, had a temple or shrine, a place that they inhabited, where they would dine off the sacrifices that people brought them. Ancient Judaism believed that the divine presence dwelt in the Jerusalem Temple.

But just building a Temple in which to offer sacrifices is not what God really wanted. The Temple was a visible symbol of Israelite faith, but as the prophet Isaiah makes clear:

> 'What need have I of all your sacrifices?' says the Lord. 'I have had enough of your burnt offerings of rams, and the fat of fed animals and I do not delight in the blood of bulls and lambs and he-goats … Learn to do well, seek justice, relieve the oppressed, be just to the orphan, plead for the widow.'[26]

The rebuke that Cohen receives for rebuilding the Temple is because, when it stood, its pilgrims simply went through the formal motions of religious worship. They performed the rituals correctly, but their spirits were lacking. Often, according to the biblical prophets, they abandoned God altogether and returned to idol worship. As a result the Temple was destroyed and the divine presence departed.[27]

The divine presence, known as the *Shechinah*, is imagined in Jewish mythology as a radiant light. Someone on whom the divine light shines is described as 'receiving the face of the *Shechinah*'.[28] Conversely, when the divine presence withdraws, it is as if God has hidden his face. The rebuke to Cohen is that, by adhering to a formal, soulless religion, practising empty rituals, eschewing justice and good deeds, he has covered up

God's face. He can't change his name and obtain a new destiny until he has first put right the errors that have led him to his current state.

And so the song ends with a prayer. That the song's spirit might '**rise up pure and free. May it be a shield for you, a shield against the enemy**.'

Cohen wrote and sang the song to the Israeli soldiers. But he is singing it in the first person, as a dialogue between himself and his father. He may have sung it for the soldiers, but it is about him. Leonard Cohen strove to make all his work personal. Nearly 20 years after he wrote *Lover, Lover, Lover* he said: 'I don't think my writing has got personal enough yet … when it's really personal everybody understands it. There is a middle ground which is just unzipping and self-indulgence, but when you really tell the truth people immediately perceive that.'[29]

INTERLUDE: LEONARD COHEN THE *COHEN*

Leonard Cohen had a hereditary connection to prayer. His name declared that it was so.

Many people have a surname, like Smith, Baker or Taylor, which indicates the occupation of one of their ancestors. So does the surname Cohen, but rather differently. Mr or Mrs Baker or Taylor is not necessarily a baker or a tailor today. But most people called Cohen are not just descended from a *cohen* (plural: *cohenim*) they are also *cohenim* themselves. As were all their ancestors.

Cohen is the Hebrew word for a priest. Not necessarily a Jewish priest, the mysterious biblical character Melchizedek is referred to as a *cohen*, and he lived long before there were any Jews. The first Jewish *cohen* was Moses' brother Aaron, and all priestly *cohenim* today are theoretically descended from him. (To complicate things though, there are however some people called Cohen who aren't *cohenim*, and there are many *cohenim* who have different surnames.) The Cohen families are a clan within the tribe of Levi. The Levites are one of the twelve ancient tribes of Israel, the only one to have still retained its identity today.

In biblical times, and for some centuries thereafter, a male Cohen had a very clearly defined role. It was his job to minister in the Sanctuary, to offer the sacrifices that the Israelites brought. He was assisted by the other members of the tribe of Levi, those who weren't *cohenim*. In return for their sacred duties the *cohenim* and Levites were supported by the rest of the nation, who gave them a proportion of their harvests and flocks. This support was important because, unlike the other tribes, the Levites and *cohenim* were not given their own territory in the Land of Israel.

The ancient *cohenim*, the biblical priests, were considered to be the nation's sages. 'For the lips of the *cohen* preserve knowledge,' says the prophet Malachi, 'and they will seek Torah from his mouth.'[30] If someone was feared to have succumbed to the biblical plague that is translated as 'leprosy' (it's a mistranslation), it was the *cohen* who was called to diagnose it. If the *cohen* declared that the patient was indeed suffering from the malady, they were put into quarantine, not to be released until the *cohen* confirmed that they had recovered. Only a *cohen* could do this; if anyone else diagnosed a patient as suffering from this illness, they would be ignored. The *cohen* was holy, and it was this sanctity that bestowed wisdom upon him.[31]

When the Jerusalem Temple was destroyed in the year 70 CE, the *cohen*'s cultic role came to an end. There were no more sacrifices in Judaism, and the Temple *cohenim* became redundant. But two rituals remained, one of which Leonard Cohen certainly performed. It is based on the blessing in the book of Numbers which the priests are to bestow on the Israelite nation: 'May the Lord bless you and keep you. May the Lord make his face shine upon you and be gracious to you. May the Lord lift up his face to you and grant you peace.' It sounds more striking in Hebrew, composed of three sentences of three, five and seven words respectively, ending in the evocative word *shalom*.[32]

This blessing is still recited in synagogues today. The *cohenim* line up at the front of the room, place their prayer shawls over their head and arms, and reach out towards the congregation. They separate the fingers of each hand so that there is a gap between the thumb and first finger, and between the third and fourth fingers. Their two thumbs touch, so that in total there are five spaces between their five pairs of fingers. In his concerts, Leonard Cohen would often have a drawing of the priestly hands projected onto the backdrop. He inscribed the blessing on a Christmas card he sent to his friend the Irish author and playwright John MacKenna in 2014, accompanied by the petition 'May the Christos be born in every heart.'[33]

There is no record of Leonard Cohen ever conducting the other surviving priestly ritual, the ceremonial redemption of a first-born baby boy. The ceremony is performed by a *cohen*, to release a first-born from his ancient cultic duties. It is an unusual ceremony, because there are certain conditions that have to be fulfilled before a baby qualifies to be redeemed. It is often an opportunity for the new parents or grandparents to give a party for friends and family. They choose a *cohen* from among their friends or acquaintances and offer him five ceremonial coins in order to get their baby back. (The *cohen* can't refuse.) If Leonard Cohen ever participated in this ceremony, his biographers were never told.

In the synagogue, the *cohen* has the privilege of being the first person called to the Torah reading. But not because they are particularly holy. The custom was introduced to prevent squabbles. Being called first to the Torah is an honour, and arguments used to break out over who it should be given to. So it was decided, long ago, that a *cohen* should always be called first, to put an end to the bickering. It seems to have worked, so far.

COME HEALING
Old Ideas (2012)

Nearly half a century after his first record was issued, Leonard Cohen released the album that would prove to be his most successful so far. *Old Ideas* reached number one in a dozen countries and occupied second or third slot in several others. It was the first number one he'd had anywhere in the world, apart from Sweden, and it was the first time any of his albums had even reached the top 50 in the USA. It peaked at number three. The year was 2012. Cohen was 77 years old. He'd had trouble finding an agent in 1967 because they'd thought him too old, even then.

In *Going Home*, the opening song on the album, he offers what we might consider to be a manifesto for what he is trying to achieve with his poetry and music. His aim is 'to write a love song, An anthem of forgiving, A manual for living with defeat, A cry above the suffering.' But part of Leonard Cohen's charm is that he dilutes lofty aspirations like these with ironic, self-deprecating humour. He may speak words like a sage, he sings, like someone of vision, but really he knows nothing. He is nothing more, he says, than 'a lazy bastard living in a suit'. The title of the album is ironic too, *Old Ideas* suggesting that he has nothing new to say. He told the singer Jarvis Cocker that the ideas in the album are 'about 2,614 years old, most of them, some of them a little older and some of them fresher'.[34]

When his friend John MacKenna was working on how to commemorate the passing of some young friends, he turned to Leonard Cohen's music. When he heard the track *Come Healing* on *Old Ideas* he knew what he wanted to do. *Come Healing* is one of Cohen's most optimistic works. More than just a cry above the suffering, it is one of the few occasions when the broken pieces that litter Cohen's work feel as if they may be coming together again.

> **O gather up the brokenness**
> **And bring it to me now…**
> **….The splinters that you carry,**
> **The cross you left behind.**

The opening lines of *Come Healing* suggest that the song is not about medicinal healing, the healing of an illness. This is a healing of brokenness, of promises not dared to be vowed, of people bearing splinters. Cohen is returning to his frequent theme of cosmic fracture and necessary repair. Of putting right that which has been fractured. In *You Know Who I Am* he sang about being a broken man, whom God would teach to repair. *Come Healing* is part of that repair.

> **Come healing of the body**
> **Come healing of the mind.**

The idea that both body and mind may need healing took a long time to enter the religious consciousness. Although the dualism of mortal body and immortal soul is fundamental to Plato's philosophy, it was virtually unknown to the Bible. It wasn't until the medieval Jewish prayer book that a request was formulated for a 'complete healing, a healing of the soul and a healing of the mind'. Cohen would have been familiar with that prayer from the synagogue, although, as we would expect, he expands and develops the idea.

The Hebrew language has three separate words that can each be translated as 'soul'. This gave rise to the kabbalistic idea that the soul is divided into three parts: the life force common to all living creatures, the intellect and the divine spirit. The last two are unique to humans.

Cohen addresses each of these three aspects of the soul in turn, transforming his couplet of body and mind in later verses, first into spirit and limb, then into reason and heart.

And let the heavens hear it
The penitential hymn.

Prayers for repentance appeared in Christian and Jewish liturgy quite some time after the faiths were first established. Christianity's seven Penitential Psalms, traditionally recited during Lent, were selected in the sixth century by the Roman scholar and theologian Cassiodorus. A hundred years or so earlier, Jewish liturgical poets, known as *paytanim* (singular: *paytan*), started writing special penitential compositions, to be read on fast days and during the period leading up to the Day of Atonement. They made extensive use of Bible stories and Talmudic legends in their compositions. In a sense they anticipated Cohen. Perhaps he saw *Come Healing*, his own penitential hymn, as following the traditions of the medieval Hebrew poets.

> **Behold the gates of mercy**
> **In arbitrary space**
> **And none of us deserving**
> **The cruelty or the grace.**

By the fourth verse we know that Cohen is singing a penitential hymn to gather up the broken splinters of our shattered world. Many hymns of church and synagogue declare that we are not worthy of heavenly grace, that there is no reason why God should look favourably on us. Many proclaim that we are sinners, that in order to be redeemed or cleansed of our sin we deserve whatever trials and punishments are destined to come our way. Cohen does not: it does not accord with his Zen outlook. We do not deserve to be subjected to arbitrary punishments; we should not endure sufferings that seem to bear no relation to the intensity of our misdeeds.

The accusation that God dispenses justice in an arbitrary manner goes back to the formative days of both Christianity and modern Judaism. It was put forward by people who argued that the true God, the God of the immortal soul, had been usurped by a lesser power – known as a demiurge – who now controlled the world. The demiurge was responsible for the existence of evil; he was capricious, his justice was arbitrary.

Cohen seems to sympathize with these people, dualists as they were called. We are living in arbitrary space, cries Cohen, we don't deserve it. What we deserve is to be allowed to enter the Gates of Mercy.

If justice is arbitrary, then we should stand as much chance of being treated mercifully as of being punished. Seeing the Gates of Mercy in arbitrary space, then, is Cohen's reasoned argument that, if we are not deserving of either grace or cruelty, to be shown divine mercy is a legitimate request. But the Gate of Mercy has another, deeper meaning too.

The ancient walls of Jerusalem have eight gates. The eastern gate, facing the Mount of Olives, is known as the Golden Gate, or the Gate of Mercy. Although the existing gate only dates back to the sixth century, at the earliest, and has been sealed since 1541, it sits on the site of an older gate, one that is the subject of legend in both Jewish and Christian lore.

The second-century text, the Infancy Gospel of James says that the Gate of Mercy was where the Virgin Mary's parents met, after her mother learned she was to have a child. It was the gate through which Jesus entered Jerusalem on Palm Sunday, and it is the gate through which believers maintain he will enter the city again in the future, on his way down from the Mount of Olives. According to the prophet Ezekiel, it is the gate through which God's glory entered Jerusalem, following which it is to be permanently sealed.[35] Later Jewish tradition believes that this is the gate through which the Messiah will come at the end of time. It was given the name Gate of Mercy when the Temple still stood, because the scapegoat bearing Israel's sins was led through it into the wilderness on the Day of Atonement.

Invoking the Gates of Mercy is more for Cohen than just a poetic construction. The healing that he is calling for is that of the broken world. It is a messianic healing, a healing that will be accomplished when the Messiah, or Jesus, depending on your point of view, enters Jerusalem, the holy city, through the Eastern Gate, the Gate of Mercy.

IF IT BE YOUR WILL
Various Positions (1985)

The formula 'May It Be Your Will' is often used to introduce petitions in the Hebrew prayer book. The phrase stands at the beginning of prayers, both short and long, asking for anything from health, wisdom, good tidings, safe travel or prosperity to the rebuilding of the Temple or divine favour for completing a meritorious act. Cohen's song *If It Be Your Will* is a slightly more hesitant version of the prayer book's formula. 'May It Be Your Will' indicates that the petitioner knows that it is possible that their request will be granted; 'If It Be Your Will' suggests they are not so sure. Or, as in Cohen's opening stanza, they are uncertain what course of action is required.

> **If it be your will**
> **That I speak no more**
> **And my voice be still**
> **As it was before**
> **I will speak no more.**

When he played London's O2 arena in July 2008, Cohen told his audience that *If It Be Your Will* was 'a sort of a prayer' written 'a while ago', when he was facing some obstacles. He didn't go into detail, but when the song was first recorded, in 1984, for the *Various Positions* album, he had recently come through a severe creative block, brought about, according to one biographer, by a growing sense of mortality as he approached the age of 50.

> I found myself in my underwear crawling along the carpets
> in a shabby room at the Royalton hotel unable to nail
> a verse. And knowing that I had a recording session and
> knowing that I could get by with what I had but that I'm not
> going to be able to do it.[36]

If It Be Your Will is a personal prayer; many of its phrases have a biblical resonance, but none is a direct quote from scripture. Struggling with his creativity, unable to compose his verse, he asks if he should silence his voice and sing no longer. There is a trace in this of the meditation sung by the prayer leader in the synagogue on the Day of Atonement, in an introduction to the most intense part of the service. In hyperbolic language the prayer leader declares his unworthiness for his sacred task, for the responsibility placed on him. He asks that his voice be heard, that there be no impediment to his prayers and that they ascend to the heavenly throne. Cohen may have intended his opening lines as a sort of reflection on this prayer, his request spoken from the heart rather than formulaically recited from the liturgy.

> **All your praises they shall ring**
> **If it be your will**
> **To let me sing**
> **From this broken hill.**

The humility of the first verse gives way to a growing sense of confidence as the song proceeds, a trust that he is making his requests in the right way. Perhaps, Cohen ventures, the divine will is that he may after all sing, provided he does so with a true voice. The language sounds biblical, but the construction of the phrases is quintessentially Cohen: praises ring out continually in his work, particularly in the psalm-like *Book of Mercy*. He frequently mentions hills, and many times he sings of things that are broken, awaiting repair. There is no specifically broken hill in the Bible, but there are a few candidates; desolate mounds on the sites of razed cities, or the hill at Golgotha where Jesus was crucified. 'The earth is wholly broken,' declares Isaiah. 'The mountains melt like wax,' says the psalmist.[37]

The sense of confidence continues to grow as Cohen's trust in the efficacy of his humility increases. If it be the divine will, the third verse continues, then the broken hills will rejoice, the rivers will fill. The language reflects the Bible more closely: 'The rivers will clap hands, together the mountains will rejoice.'[38] God's mercy will spill:

On all these burning hearts in hell
If it be your will, to make us well.

Cohen's uncertainty over whether he should speak is transforming into a petition for healing. And now Cohen is able to give his prayer a universal significance. He started by wondering whether he should stop speaking; now he believes he has garnered enough divine favour to allow him to pray for the whole of humanity.

> **And draw us near**
> **And bind us tight**
> **All your children here**
> **In their rags of light.**

'Rags of light' are mentioned in the Bible when Adam and Eve are expelled from the Garden of Eden. They were naked in the Garden, so when God threw them out, into the world, he made clothes for them out of animal skin. A variant spelling in an ancient Torah scroll spelled the Hebrew word for skin with a different first letter. It sounded the same, but instead of reading 'clothes of skin' it read 'clothes of light'. The Jewish mystical tradition seized on this idea. Originally, says the Zohar, the clothes were made of light, but after Adam and Eve sinned they were transformed into clothes of animal skin. Cohen has the human race still dressed in their primitive, primordial glory, garbed in rags of light, seeking to be drawn close to God.[39]

If It Be Your Will has the same intention as the prayer leader's request on the Day of Atonement. Having declared his unworthiness, the prayer leader asks for his failings to be overlooked and for his requests on behalf of the congregation to be accepted: 'help me succeed ... in seeking mercy for myself and for those who have appointed me ... that you listen to the prayers of your people in mercy.' Of course, Cohen was not appointed to the job of praying on behalf of the community, so we can't extend the comparison too far. But the synagogue prayer is known by its opening word, *Hineni*, 'Here I Am'. It is the word with which Abraham responded when he received the summons that would tell him to crucify his son. It is the word that Cohen will introduce into the global cultural lexicon in his final album, in the song *You Want It Darker*, which anticipates his impending death.

Hineni, 'Here I Am,' cries the man praying on behalf of the community on the Day of Atonement, the most solemn day in the calendar. 'Here I Am,' cries Abraham on the most traumatic, devastating day of his life. And 'Here I Am,' Cohen will one day cry, as he prepares to depart this world. Here I am; if it be your Will.

YOU WANT IT DARKER
You Want It Darker (2016)

Leonard Cohen had grown old. He could no longer perform; years of dancing around the stage, of falling to his knees before the audience, were demanding payback. He had problems with his spine, and he had been diagnosed with cancer. He was still working though. He had started another album, but recording was in abeyance. He was no longer able to climb the stairs to the studio. His son Adam recognized that the work had to carry on; it was necessary for his father's recovery, indeed for his survival.

Adam set up a studio in his father's living room and took over the production of the album, with Cohen singing from his chair. Some days he could only work for an hour or two, but there were days when he would rise out of his chair and dance.

Cohen called the album *You Want It Darker*. The first track on the album has the same title, an ironic one from someone whose music had often been considered gloomy and heavy-hearted, even if it was no longer called 'music to kill yourself by'. The song's title wasn't addressed to his listeners. And it wasn't a query: there is no question mark following *You Want It Darker*. Rather, the title summed up his lifelong difficulty with the power whose presence he felt so strongly, the power that seemed to desire suffering in the world.

The album was released on 21 October 2016. A week earlier Cohen had attended the album's formal launch at the official residence of Canada's Consul General in Los Angeles. He'd heard Adam Cohen speak about producing the album and express his admiration for his father, the transcendent value he injected into his work, his tireless success, marvelled at by those who watched him from the sidelines.

Among the guests at the album's launch was Gideon Zelermyer, Cantor of the Shaar Hashomayim synagogue in Montreal, the congregation that Cohen had attended as a child, where his grandfather and great-grandfather had both been president. Accompanied by the synagogue's choir, Zelermyer's voice can be heard in a solo, cantorial rendition of the single word *hineni* at the end of *You Want It Darker*.

Hineni – 'Here I am' – is Cohen's poignant response to the God he hears calling him at the end of his life. As for Abraham when commanded to sacrifice his son, or Moses at the Burning Bush, or Jacob on his journey into the unknown, *hineni* is the submissive response to a summons from the deity. Leonard Cohen had heard the summons. He knew he was on his way. But there were still things he had to say, before he went.

If you are the dealer, I am out of the game
If you are the healer, I'm broken and lame
If thine is the glory then mine must be the shame
You want it darker
We kill the flame.[40]

You Want It Darker is an accusation, a rebuke to the power who deals the cards, heals the lame, radiates glory and, despite all this, condemns us to extinguish the flame. Fire and flame were always present in Leonard Cohen's work, pursuing *Joan of Arc*, burning on his heart is *Born in Chains*, ascending into the sun in *The Window*, sealing fates in *Who by Fire*. It is no coincidence that *The Flame* is the title of the final collection of Cohen's poetry, published posthumously but for which he made selections before he died. '**We kill the flame**,' he sang: we extinguish the light because of you, the dealer, the healer, the glory, who wants it darker. Cohen had had enough. He wanted out of the game.

> **Magnified and sanctified, be Thy Holy Name,**
> **Vilified and crucified, in the human frame,**
> **A million candles burning for the help that never**
> **came,**
> **You want it darker.**
> *Hineni Hineni*
> **I'm ready, my Lord.**

The first line of the chorus is the opening words of the Kaddish, the Jewish prayer recited by bereaved relatives during their statutory period of mourning.

> Magnified, sanctified, be the holy name
> In the world that he created by his will.
> And may he establish his kingdom
> In your lives and in your days and in the lives of the whole
> house of Israel
> Speedily and very soon.

Often wrongly described as a prayer for the dead, the Kaddish is a doxology, an exhortation to praise the God whose deeds far surpass our understanding. And to express the hope that the divine kingdom will be speedily established on earth.

Cohen quotes only the first words of the Kaddish; he sanctifies the Holy Name, the Name he has so often sung about. But he is not ready to advocate for the divine kingdom to be established on earth. Instead his Kaddish morphs into a condemnation of humanity for vilifying God's name, and for crucifying Christ in his human frame.

And, by implication, a censure of God for allowing it to happen, for wanting it darker. The '**million candles burning**' signifies any genocide you choose; Cohen almost certainly had the Holocaust in mind, although one million is only a fraction of the total. His anger is palpable: he recites the Kaddish for the dead but reserves his censure for the divinity who wants it darker. And then, since there is nothing more he can do, other than serve the power whose ways he cannot understand, he declares *hineni* – here I am. I am ready.

Hineni, that declaration of readiness no matter what the outcome, that's a part of everyone's soul. We all are motivated by deep impulses and deep appetites to serve, even though we may not be able to locate that which we are willing to serve. So, this is just a part of my nature, and I think everybody else's nature, to offer oneself at the moment, at the critical moment when the emergency becomes articulate. It's only when the emergency becomes articulate that we can locate that willingness to serve.[41]

It's not all bad though, as he acknowledges in the second verse.

> **There's a lover in the story …**
> **There's a lullaby for suffering …**
> **But it's written in the scriptures**
> **And it's not some idle claim.**

There is love, and suffering can be assuaged. But the scriptures told us long ago that it was going to be like this; '**You want it darker**' is not an idle claim.

Finally, Cohen acknowledges that, compared with what it could have been, his life has been easy. His next verse begins with prisoners being lined up in front of a firing squad, but that wasn't his life.

> **… I struggled with some demons**
> **They were middle-class and tame**
> **Didn't know I had permission**
> **To murder and to maim**
> **You want it darker**
> **We kill the flame.**

His life had been troubled by demons but, he has to admit, they were mild: 'middle-class and tame'. He never knew that he could have acted differently, that he could have crossed over to the side of evil, '**to murder and to maim**'. Had he realized sooner that the divinity wanted it darker, who knows what sort of life he might have had?

You Want It Darker was far from the only song in which Cohen accused God of injustice and cruelty. He did so in *The Butcher* and *Amen*, where again his accusation was of permitting an environment in which the Holocaust could happen. But there is a capitulation in *You Want It Darker* that we don't find in his other accusatory pieces. It is the capitulation of *hineni*, of readiness to submit to the final judgement of eternity.

In the final interview that he gave, Cohen told David Remnick that the purpose of prayer was to remind God that before the catastrophe at creation there was a harmonious unity. It sounds like chutzpah, daring to speak about God in such a way. But it reflects Cohen's profound spirituality, a spirituality that is predicated on a dynamic partnership with God, one in which each party has a role to play. Cohen's was to repair the broken world in which he found himself, a world swarming with demons, however middle-class and tame. And God's was to make his presence felt, to create and sustain the world that Cohen was obliged to repair.

I know there's a spiritual aspect to everybody's life, whether they want to cop to it or not. It's there, you can feel it in people – there's some recognition that there is a reality that they cannot penetrate but which influences their mood and activity. So that's operating. That activity at certain points of your day or night insists on a certain kind of response.

Sometimes it's just like: 'You are losing too much weight, Cohen. You're dying, but you don't have to cooperate enthusiastically with the process. Force yourself to have a sandwich.'

What I mean to say is that you hear the *Bat Kol* [divine voice] ...You hear this other deep reality singing to you all the time, and much of the time you can't decipher it. Even when I was healthy, I was sensitive to the process. At this stage of the game, I hear it saying, 'Cohen, just get on with the things you have to do.' It's very compassionate at this stage. More than at any time of my life, I no longer have that voice that says, 'You're fucking up.' That's a tremendous blessing, really.

Spiritual things, *baruch hashem* [Blessed be the Name], have fallen into place, for which I am deeply grateful.[42]

EPILOGUE – A MODERN-DAY
PAYTAN?

Some time around the fifth or sixth century a new form of poetry began to be written in the land of Israel. Elaborate and scholarly, the poems were usually written by prayer leaders, with the intention of chanting or singing them as additions to the regular prayers. It was a skilful task. Each poem had to reflect the theme of the prayer that it accompanied. It had to be of a sufficiently high standard for the congregation to appreciate its literary qualities, rather than growing restless at having to listen to something they didn't want to hear.

Each poem was known as a *piyyut*; the composer was a *paytan*. Some of their compositions are still recited today.

One of the features of this poetry was that it was packed with allusions to biblical stories and folklore. A successful *paytan* knew the Bible inside out, and had a masterly grasp of all the fables and legends with which later generations had embellished it. Like Leonard Cohen, the *paytan* took ancient fables and legends and made them relevant to the world they lived in, to the congregation listening to his composition. Hearing someone recite a *piyyut* in the Middle Ages must have been a bit like listening to a Leonard Cohen song today.

Indeed, in some ways Leonard Cohen was a modern-day *paytan*. Of course he didn't set out to write music for religious worship, but his songs have found their way into both church and synagogue services, and into religious ceremonies that are not part of the established religions.

In May 2016 the Irish author and playwright John MacKenna emailed Leonard Cohen. John had been a friend of Cohen for over 30 years, since producing a radio interview with him in 1985 for the RTE Ireland programme *Favourite Five*. MacKenna told Cohen that in the spring and early summer that year three young friends of his had died, two by suicide and one in an accident. He wanted to remember them and to do something that might bring some sense of comfort to their families. As a writer, he thought about how he might do this and he came up with idea of a stage requiem in the form of a Mass.

He asked Cohen whether he could use his poems, music and writings to create the requiem. He didn't want to use material from anywhere else. It would be a requiem by Leonard Cohen.

I approached Leonard – with whom I'd been friends for more than thirty years – with the idea of shaping a Mass from his work with all of the spoken word coming from his texts.

His initial reaction was that the Catholic Mass was a very sacred and important work and he felt it would be challenging. His second reaction came from his droll sense of humour and made me smile. He said, 'I'm a Buddhist Jew, you're an agnostic Quaker, how are we supposed to write a Catholic Mass?' But he gave the go-ahead and over that summer I sent various ideas to him, put together several versions of the text until we were both happy with the completed version.[1]

And so the task began.

Over a period of several months I reread his written work and listened again and again to the songs — from the first album to *You Want It Darker*. Cohen's songs and poems and prose are littered with Jewish, Buddhist and Christian imagery but they are brimming, too, with love, loss, passion, tragedy, compassion and hope.[2]

As the Requiem began to take shape, Cohen was growing ill. He told his manager, Robert Kory, how touched he felt that John could find the elements of a sacred requiem within his work. He asked Robert to assist, should rights approval become an issue, so that the work could be widely performed.

Two weeks before his death on 7 November 2016, Cohen approved the final draft of the requiem. Sadly he did not live to see its premiere, which took place in the Irish town of Carlow on 15 June the following year. The Irish President, Michael D. Higgins, was there, as was the Canadian ambassador to Ireland, Kevin Vickers.

The requiem is the most ambitious liturgical use of Cohen's work, but it is far from being the only one. *Who by Fire*, the song based on the Day of Atonement liturgy, has been recited in many synagogues, either as an accompaniment to the Hebrew original or even in place of it. When the Reform synagogue movement decided to produce a new prayer book for the Day of Atonement, they printed *Who by Fire* as a study text to accompany the Hebrew prayer.[3] Some synagogues sing *Hallelujah*, *Story of Isaac* or *If It Be Your Will* during services, or dedicate shabbat study events to celebrations of Cohen's music. Others set psalms and prayers to the tune of *Hallelujah*.

Although synagogues often display an almost proprietorial relationship with Cohen's music – he was, after all Jewish – his music is used just as frequently in Christian circles. His lyrics have been sung in services and at weddings and funerals. *Hallelujah*, far and away the most liturgically popular of his compositions, is regularly sung in church services, sometimes to new lyrics or even adapted to fit ancient hymns, like the Easter sequence, *Victimae paschali laudes*. A church in Toronto held an evening Eucharist featuring Cohen's music; others have held Leonard Cohen evenings or events dedicated to his work.

Leonard Cohen once said that he saw himself as the priest of a catacomb religion, one that developed underground and was better attuned than the established religions to the needs and priorities of the modern world. It was a remark he made at the beginning of his musical career; the ambition didn't come to fruition, and he never mentioned it again. He was, however, frequently referred to, by fans and journalists, as a prophet, a role he'd imposed on himself 1963, when he castigated the local community in his speech at the Montreal Jewish Public Library. He'd condemned their lack of spirituality and told them that they needed a prophet.

But being a prophet is a lofty ambition, one that does not sit well with a man of Cohen's humility. He wanted to heal but he did not, as a Hebrew prophet must, seek to repair the brokenness of the world through dire prognostications and threats of doom.

Leonard Cohen brought comfort to many, smoothed the path to healing and shone a beacon of spiritual light upon the world. Yet if he was neither catacomb priest nor prophet, how should we think of him? He could be a psalmist, a poet, lover and musician in the mould of King David, but he was a *cohen*, a member of the Jewish priestly tribe, and the Talmud tells us that a *cohen* cannot be a king.

That leaves us with a *paytan*, a scholarly musician and poet, a prayer leader imbued in the religious traditions with a profound knowledge of Bible and Talmudic lore. Even though he did not deliberately compose liturgical music, his work found its way into church and synagogue. It would not be too outrageous to think of Leonard Cohen as a contemporary liturgical poet, as a modern-day *paytan*.

Which leaves us with a question. Contemporary music is ephemeral. Leonard Cohen's music has already survived far longer than most of his musical contemporaries. But the work of some of the early *paytanim* has survived for over a thousand years. The question is, when modern music has run its course, will Leonard Cohen still be a *paytan*?

ACKNOWLEDGEMENTS

The idea came for this book came when I was driving along the A40 towards the North Circular and *Hallelujah* came onto the radio. Like many of us, I knew the song well, but for some reason I listened to the lyrics a little more carefully than usual. A penny dropped when I heard about King David's secret chord, and as I listened more closely I realized that the song was crammed full of allusions to biblical and rabbinic mythology. So I am grateful to whoever the DJ was who played *Hallelujah* at that time; unfortunately I don't remember the date, time or even the radio station. But I'm sure you know who you are.

More specifically, I am grateful to the biographers and scholars whose work was invaluable in helping me to write this book. To Ira Nadel, Sylvie Simmons and Jeff Burger, whose volumes were constant companions. To Jarkko Arjatsalo, whose website leonardcohenfiles.com is a tremendous resource, immaculately constructed and more comprehensive than one could possibly imagine. To John MacKenna for telling me about the requiem he wrote with Leonard Cohen, and to Leonard Cohen's manager, Robert Kory, who generously guided me through the process of gaining permissions to reproduce his lyrics. I am also, of course, grateful to Katie Cacouris and Tucker Smith of The Wylie Agency for their help with permissions, to David Beal of Special Rider Music, Victoria Fox of Farrar, Straus and Giroux and Kate Pool at the Society of Authors.

As always, this book would not have been possible without the support of my wife, Karen, who encouraged the idea of the book from the outset and challenged me when she thought I was getting too carried away. And of course my wonderful publishers at Bloomsbury Continuum: Robin Baird-Smith, Jamie Birkett, Julia Mitchell, Amy Greaves, Rosie Parnham, Penny Liechti and Rachel Nicholson, who I never manage to thank properly for their confidence, encouragement and positivity. This is now the fifth Bloomsbury book I have written, and on every one they have been a pleasure and a delight to work with.

PERMISSIONS

NOTES

FOREWORD

1   Tikkunei Zohar 26b.

INTRODUCTION

1   *Otzar Ta'amei Hazal.* The English title page inaccurately translates it as *Thesaurus of Talmudical Interpretations.* It contains, according to the title page, 'all the interpretations of the Pentateuch, as given in the Talmudim, Tosefta, Mechilta, Sifra, Sifre, Pesiktot, Midrash Rabba, Tanhuma and other Midrashim'.

2   Unkempt, scruffy.

3   Winifried Siemerling, 'Leonard Cohen. Loneliness and History: A Speech Before the Jewish Public Library', in *Take This Waltz: A Celebration of Leonard Cohen*, ed. Michael Fournier and Ken Norris (Ste Anne de Bellevue, Quebec: Muses Co., 1994), pp. 143–53.

4   Sandra Djwa, 'After the Wipeout, a Renewal', *The Ubyssey,* 7 February 1967. https://open.library.ubc.ca/collections/ubc publications/ubysseynews/items/1.0125993#p7z-4rof:cohen

5   Ibid.

6   Ibid.

7   Interview with Robert Sward, Malahat Review, December 1984 quoted in Burger, *Leonard Cohen on Leonard Cohen* (Chicago: Chicago Review Press, 2014).

8   'Leonard Cohen: His Last Interview (Complete)', David Remnick, 6 November 2017, https://www.youtube.com/watch?v=BVpG3tOonOQ

9   *Song of Leonard Cohen*, documentary by Harry Rasky, 1980.

1 LEONARD COHEN'S INFLUENCES

1 Interview with Kristine McKenna, *L.A. Weekly*, March 1988, quoted in Burger, *Leonard Cohen on Leonard Cohen*, p. 200.

2 'Porridge, Lozenge, Syringe', interview with Adrian Deevoy, *Q Magazine*, 1991, https://www.leonardcohenfiles.com/qmag.html

3 Agreta Wirberg and Stina Dabrowski, *Stina möter Leonard Cohen (Stina meets Leonard Cohen)*, Swedish TV film, 1997, quoted in Sylvie Simmons, *I'm Your Man: The Life of Leonard Cohen* (Vintage, 2013), p. 350.

4 Interview with Alberto Manzano, *El Europeo*, Spring 1993, quoted in Burger, *Leonard Cohen on Leonard Cohen*, p. 326.

5 '"I am the little Jew who wrote the Bible" – A Conversation between Leonard Cohen and Arthur Kurzweil', 23 November 1993, https://www.leonardcohenfiles.com/arthurkurzweil.pdf.

6 *Toronto Star*, 18 October 1986 quoted in Ira Nadel, *Various Positions: A Life of Leonard Cohen* (Toronto: Random House of Canada, 1995), p. 23.

7 Interview with Elizabeth Boleman-Herring, *The Athenian*, September 1988, quoted in Burger, *Leonard Cohen on Leonard Cohen*, p. 232.

8 'Five hundred readers': Louis Dudek Papers, quoted on http://canpoetry.library.utoronto.ca/dudek/index.htm. 'Among the great': Christian Fevret, *Les Inrockuptibles*, 21 August 1991, quoted in Simmons, *I'm Your Man*, p. 39.

9 Desmond Pacey, *Culture*, December 1958, quoted in Nadel, *Various Positions*, p. 66.

10 Liel Leibovitz, *A Broken Hallelujah: Rock and Roll, Redemption, and the Life of Leonard Cohen* (New York: W.W. Norton, 2014), pp. 83–5.

11 Interview with Pat Harbron, *Beetle*, December 1973, quoted in Burger, *Leonard Cohen on Leonard Cohen*, p. 50.

12 Nadel, *Various Positions*, p. 210.

13 Leonard Cohen, 'Final Revision of My Life in Art', unpublished manuscript, p. 85, quoted in Nadel, *Various Positions*, p. 211.

14 'Songs and Thoughts of Leonard Cohen', interview with Robert O'Brian, January 1987, http://robertobrianinterviews.blogspot.com/2011/12/Cohen-cohen.html

15 Christian Fevret, *Les Inrockuptibles* 21 August 1991, quoted in Nadel, *Various Positions*, p. 70.

16 Jeremy Robson, 'Transitional', *Jewish Quarterly*, 20(3), Autumn 1972, p. 47.

17 Interview with Robin Pike, *ZigZag*, October 1974, https://www.Cohencohenforum.com/viewtopic.php?t=20064

18 Mort Rosengarten, quoted in Simmons, *I'm Your Man*, p. 46.

19 Leonard Cohen, 'Final Revision of My Life in Art', unpublished manuscript, quoted in Nadel, *Various Positions* p. 196.

20 Interview with Robin Pike, *ZigZag*.

21 Leibovitz, *A Broken Hallelujah*, p. 101.

22 'How the Heart Approaches What It Yearns', radio interview with John MacKenna, RTE Ireland, 9 May 1988, transcribed by Martin Godwyn, https://www.leonardcohenfiles.com/rte.html.

23 Ibid.

24 Alastair Pirrie, 'Cohen Regrets', *New Musical Express*, 10 March 1973, accessed at https://www.leonardcohenfiles.com/nme2.html

2 THE BIBLE AS ALLEGORY

1 Ruth 1.16.

2 Radio interview with Kristine McKenna, March 1988; Kristine McKenna, 'Eight Hours to Harry', radio interview, October 1988, *KCRW-FM*; Burger, *Leonard Cohen on Leonard Cohen*, p. 243.

3 H. Rasky, *The Song of Leonard Cohen: A Portrait of a Poet, a Friendship and a Film* (Oakville: Mosaic Press, 2001), p. 74.

4 Gen. 22.1–19.

5 Solomon Klonitzky-Kline, *Otzar Ta'amei Hazal* (New York: Shulsinger, 1939), p. 101.

6 Sanhedrin 89b.

7 Genesis Rabbah 56,3.

8 'How the Heart Approaches What It Yearns'.

9 Simmons, *I'm Your Man*, p. 194.

10 Interview with Robin Pike, *Zigzag*.

11 Exod. 3.13.

12 John 1.14.

13 Matthew 26.17–18.

14 Rev. 7.14.

15 Federico García Lorca, 'Sonnet of the Sweet Complaint', 'The Gipsy-Nun'.

16 'How the Heart Approaches what it Yearns'.

17. Quoted in Tim de Lisle, 'Who Held a Gun to Leonard Cohen's Head?, *The Guardian*, 27 September 2004.

18 The Hasmoneans, who ruled Israel between the third and first centuries BCE, were both priests and kings. It was as a result of their corrupt reign that the Romans occupied Israel, crucifying Jesus, destroying the Jerusalem Temple and creating the conditions for much of subsequent world history.

19 1 Sam. 16.13.

20 Berachot 3b, B'midbar Rabba 15,16, Midrash Tehillim 22 et al.

21 Pesahim 117a.

22 2 Sam. 11.1 ff.

23 Sanhedrin 107a.

24 2 Sam. 18.9.

25 Mishnah Sotah 1:8.

26 Exod. 20.7.

27 Mt. 26.65; Lev. 24.10–12; 2 Sam. 12.10.

28 Num. 20.7–11.

29 Zohar 1:6b. The scholarly view is that the Zohar was compiled in Castile in the latter half of the thirteenth century. The book itself claims to have been written in the Land of Israel in the second century, a view still held by many orthodox scholars. For other legends about the staff, see *Pirkei d'Rabbi Eliezer*, 40 and *Tanna d'Be Eliyahu Zuta, Perek Yeridot*, 2.

30 Gen. 1.3.

31 Jn 1.1.

32 Rosh Hashanah 16b.

33 Harry Rasky, dir., *Song of Leonard Cohen* (1980).

34 CBS Radio interview with Robert Sward, December 1984; reproduced in Burger, *Leonard Cohen on Leonard Cohen*.

35 Jiří Měsíc, 'The Nature of Love in the Work of Leonard Cohen', *Journal of Popular Romance Studies*, October 2018, http://www.jprstudies.org/2018/10/the-nature-of-love-in-the-work-of-Cohen-cohenby-jiri-mesic/.

36 https://www.youtube.com/watch?v=cSV6_JzHbu8

37 Exodus Rabbah 1,26.

38 Yoma 57a.

39 Ps. 137.2–3.

40 Ps. 137.4–9.

41 Rev. 17.4–18.3.

42 Thomas Erber, interview, *L'Optimum*, October 2001, https://www.Cohencohensite.com/10newsongs/optimum.htm.

43 Sandra Djwa, *The Ubyssey*.

44 The correct translation is 'may my right hand forget', but Cohen, in common with many translators, understands it as 'may my right hand wither'.

45 Exod. 6.12; Deut. 10.16.

46 Erber, interview, *L'Optimum*.

47 Interview with Steve Appleford, *Rolling Stone*, 11 September 2014; https://www.rollingstone.com/music/music-live-reviews/Cohen-cohen-offers-rare-peek-into-his-process-at-popular-problems-preview-76635/

48 Exod. 14.15–16.

49 Megillah 10b.

50 Mishnah Pirkei Avot 6,2.

51 Exod. 20.2 and 20.17, Targum pseudo-Jonathan, loc. cit.

52 Mishnah Pesahim 10,5.

53 Zech. 14.9.

54 Thom Jurek, 'The Prophet of Love Looks into the Abyss', interview, *Metro Times*, 18 August 1993, quoted in Burger, *Leonard Cohen on Leonard Cohen*, p. 366.

55 Gen. 49.1; Bereshit Rabbah 98,2.

56 Judg. 16.6.

57 Judg. 16.15.

58 Rita Houston, 'The Crack in Everything Lets the Light In: Leonard Cohen in New York', NPR, 25 January 2012; https://www.npr.org/sections/allsongs/2012/01/25/145842208/the-crack-in-everything-lets-the-light-in-Cohen-cohen-in-new-york

3 IDEAS FROM THE BIBLE

1 Sandra Djwa, *The Ubyssey*.

2 John Hammond, interview with Leonard Cohen, BBC, 20 September 1986; https://www.leonardcohenfiles.com/jhammond.html

3 Nadel, *Various Positions*, p. 110.

4 Radio interview with Jarvis Cocker, BBC 6 Music, 29 January 2012; https://leonardcohenfiles.com/jarvis-iv.pdf

5 Simmons, *I'm Your Man*, p. 138.

6 Interview with Kevin Howlett, BBC Radio One, 7 August 1994, quoted in Simmons, *I'm Your Man*, p. 125.

7 Harry Rasky, dir., *The Song of Leonard Cohen*.

8 The history of Mar Matthew and Mar Andrew, the Blessed Apostles, in W. Wright, *Apocryphal Acts of the Apostles* (London: Williams and Norgate, 1871), vol. 2, pp. 93–115; http://www.earlychristian-writings.com/fathers/apocryphal_acts_05_matthew_andrew.html

9 Live concert, date unknown https://www.youtube.com/watch?v=tIssqxixYpo

10 Leibovitz, *A Broken Hallelujah*, p. 34.

11 Susan Lumsden, *Weekend Magazine*, 12 September 1970, quoted in Nadel, *Various Positions*, p. 180.

12 Rev. 17.4–6.

13 Album notes, *Best of Leonard Cohen* (1975).

14 The designation of Torah as Law comes from the Septuagint, the early Greek translation of the Hebrew Bible dating from the third century BCE. It translates Torah as *nomos*, meaning 'law'.

15 'Great Missionary Arm', in Bruce Meyer and Brian O'Riordan, *In Their Words: Interviews with Fourteen Canadian Writers* (Toronto: Anansi, 1984), p. 37. 'Never left the Church', from Leonard Cohen, *Stranger Music Selected Poems and Songs* (Toronto: McClelland & Stewart, 1993), p. 265. 'Part Catholic', from Mark Rowland, 'Leonard Cohen's Nervous Breakthrough', *Musician*, July 1988, quoted in Nadel, *Various Positions*, p. 15.

16 Robert Kory, *Requiem Booklet*, 2017; https://www.leonardco-henfiles.com/requiem2017.pdf

17 Deut. 4.34.

18 'Sacrificial birds', Mishnah Pirkei Avot 3,18; 'infuriating presumption': Leonard Cohen, *Death of a Lady's Man* (Toronto: McClelland & Stewart, 1978); 'Anyone who says I am not a Jew…', Leonard Cohen, *Book of Longing* (Toronto: McClelland & Stewart, 2006), p. 158. TV interview with Stina Lundberg Dabrowski, 2001, Burger, *Leonard Cohen on Leonard Cohen*, p. 474.

19 Jon Pareles, 'At Lunch with Leonard Cohen', *The New York Times*, 11 October 1995.

20 Meyer and O'Riordan, *In Their Words: Interviews with Fourteen Canadian Writers*, p. 37.

21 Winfried Siemerling, 'A Political Constituency That Really Exists' in *Take This Waltz*, ed. Fournier and Norris.

22 Jon Pareles, 'Final Reckonings, a Tuneful Fedora and Forgiveness', interview, *The New York Times*, 27 January 2012.

23 Ps. 37.11; Mt. 5.7 and 11.29; Num. 12.3.

24 Isa. 1.10; Jer. 2.4; Ezek. 37.4 and elsewhere.

25 Klonitzky-Kline, *Otzar Ta'amei Hazal*, pp. 20–22.

26 Hullin 60b; Bereshit Rabbah 6,3.

27 Mt. 23.15.

28 Jean-Luc Esse, radio interview, *Synergie*, France-Inter, 6 October 1997; https://www.leonardcohenfiles.com/finter.html.

29 Meyer and O'Riordan, *In Their Words: Interviews with Fourteen Canadian Writers*, p. 37.

30 Howard Sounes, *Down the Highway: The Life of Bob Dylan* (New York: Grove Press, 2001).

4 Heaven and Earth

1 Interview with Leonard Cohen, CBC, 26 August 1995.

2 Simmons, *I'm Your Man* p. 225.

3 Ibid.

4 Exod. 3.14.

5 Gen. 3.9; Rashi, loc. cit. *Derekh Eretz Rabba* 5. Cf. A. J. Heschel, *God In Search of Man* (New York: Harper & Row, 1966).

6 Eccl. 10.20.

7 Eccl. 2.24.

8 Jean-Luc Esse, radio interview, France-Inter, 6 October 1997; https://www.leonardcohenfiles.com/finter.html.

9 Eccl. 1.4–9.

10 Isa. 43.18.

11 https://www.leonardcohenfiles.com/arthurkurzweil.pdf

12 Tikkunei Zohar 83b.

13 Mt. 3.16; Lk. 3.22.

14 Eccl. 3.8.

15 Mk 1.10–11; Gen. 8.8–12.

16 Paul Zollo, *Songwriters on Songwriting*, expanded edition (New York: Da Capo Press 1997); https://www.leonardcohenfiles.com/zollo.html

17 *The Future Radio Special* CD, Sony, 1992; quoted on https://qz.com/835076/Cohen-cohens-anthem-the-story-of-the-line-there-is-a-crack-in-everything-thats-how-the-light-gets-in/

18 Heb. 10.10–14

19 Quoted in de Lisle 'Who Held a Gun to Leonard Cohen's Head?'; https://www.theguardian.com/music/2004/sep/17/2

20 Elliot R. Wolfson, 'New Jerusalem Glowing: Songs and Poems of Leonard Cohen in a Kabbalistic Key', *Kabbalah: Journal for the Study of Jewish Mystical Texts*, 15 (2006), pp. 103–53.

21 Gen. 1.2.

22 See my book *Kabbalah: Secrecy, Scandal and the Soul* (London: Bloomsbury Continuum, London, 2019), p. 117.

23 Barbara Gowdy, interview, TV Ontario, 19 November 1992, quoted in Burger, *Leonard Cohen on Leonard Cohen*, pp. 294–5.

24 Gen. 15.17; Exod. 4.3–6; Isa. 7.14; Mt. 1.23. The reference to the young woman giving birth is the subject of an ancient dispute between Jewish and Christian Bible translators over the meaning of the word *almah*. Jewish translators render it as 'young woman', Christian expositors as 'virgin'. See my book *The Murderous Histories of Bible Translations* (London: Bloomsbury Continuum, 2016), p. 16.

25 Isa. 7,14–16 and 9.5–6.

26 Sanhedrin 94a.

27 Jer. 3.8.

28 Leonard Cohen, *Book of Mercy* (Toronto: McClelland & Stewart, 1984), #27.

29 Lev. 26.30; Jer. 32.35.

30 Robert Hilburn, 'A Master's Reflections on His Music', *Los Angeles Times*, 24 September 1995; https://www.latimes.com/archives/la-xpm-1995-09-24-ca-49365-story.html

31 https://www.youtube.com/watch?v=UT7blYWCqJk

32 Stina Lundberg Dabrowski, interview, Swedish National Television, 2001, quoted in Burger, *Leonard Cohen on Leonard Cohen*.

33 Ibid.

34 Vicki Gabereau, radio interview, CBC Canada, May 1984, reprinted in Burger, *Leonard Cohen on Leonard Cohen*, p. 156.

35 Wolfson, 'New Jerusalem Glowing: Songs and Poems of Leonard Cohen in a Kabbalistic Key', p. 143, n. 149. The reference to *Stranger Music* is the 1993 edition, p. 299. However, Cohen told the film-maker Harry Rasky that he had tried many versions of that song and of the lyrics: Harry Rasky, *The Song of Leonard Cohen* (London: Souvenir Press, 2010).

36 Song 2.1. Zohar 1:1a, 1:221a, 2:189b.

37 For examples of the relationship between Sufism and Kabbalah see my book *Kabbalah: Secrecy, Scandal and the Soul*.

38 Simmons, *I'm Your Man*, p. 410.

39 https://www.leonardcohenfiles.com/enough.html. *You Have Loved Enough* was published in the 2006 collection *Book of Longing*. None of the relevant words is capitalized.

40 Mishna Yadayim 3,5.

41 Hagigah 14b.

42 Mishnah Pirkei Avot 4,1; Hagigah 15a.

43 Prov. 25.16.

5 Prayer

1 Robert Sward, interview, CBS Radio, December 1984. Reproduced in Burger, *Leonard Cohen on Leonard Cohen*.

2 Hechalot Rabbati #82.

3 H. R. Jacobus, 'The Story of Leonard Cohen's "Who By Fire", a Prayer in the Cairo Genizah, Babylonian Astrology and Related Rabbinical Texts', in W. J. Lyons and E. England, eds, *Reception History and Biblical Studies* (London: Bloomsbury Continuum, 2015), pp. 201–17.

4 Harry Rasky, dir., *The Song of Leonard Cohen;* https://www.facebook.com/Cohencohen/posts/who-by-fire-first-appeared-on-Cohens-album-new-skin-for-the-old-ceremony-about/10153654619594644/

5 Stoning is a biblical penalty, but there is no explicit mention of strangling.

6 1 Kgs 19.11-13.

7 2 Kgs 2.11.

8   Harry Rasky, dir., *The Song of Leonard Cohen*.

9   For the Kurzweil interview, see the Introduction. Nadel, *Various Positions*, p. 240.

10 Quoted in Simmons, *I'm Your Man*, p. 323.

11 Simmons, *I'm Your Man*, pp. 323–4.

12 Interview with Richard Guilliatt, December 1993, in Burger, *Leonard Cohen on Leonard Cohen*, p. 406.

13 Interview with Kristine McKenna, *L.A. Weekly*, March 1988, quoted in *Burger Leonard Cohen on Leonard Cohen*, p. 204.

14 Mt. 5, 39–40.

15 Hos. 14.2–3.

16 Hos. 14.6–7.

17 Mt. 5.41; Hos. 14.10.

18 Wolfson, 'New Jerusalem Glowing: Songs and Poems of Leonard Cohen in a Kabbalistic Key', pp. 103–53.

19 Mishnah Pirkei Avot 1,17.

20 Simmons, *I'm Your Man*, p. 262.

21 Měsíc, 'The Nature of Love in the Work of Leonard Cohen'; http://www.jprstudies.org/2018/10/the-nature-of-love-in-the-work-of-Cohen-cohenby-jiri-mesic/

22 Rosh Hashanah 16b, Gen. 17.15–16.

23 Zohar Terumah 162b–163b.

24 Bereshit Rabbah 9,7.

25 Zohar Vayera 109a and elsewhere. Bereshit Rabbah 9,7. Jurek, 'The Prophet of Love Looks into the Abyss', quoted in Burger, *Leonard Cohen on Leonard Cohen*, pp. 366–7.

26 Isa. 1.11–17.

27 Shabbat 33a, Sh'mot Rabbah 2,2.

28 Berakhot 64a.

29 Adrian Deevoy, 'Porridge? Lozenge? Syringe?', *Q*, 1991, quoted in Burger, *Leonard Cohen on Leonard Cohen*, p. 255.

30 Mal. 2.7.

31 See Lev. 13.

32 Num. 6.24–6.

33 Author correspondence with John MacKenna, September 2014.

34 Jarvis Cocker, interview, BBC 6 Music, 29 January 2012; https://leonardcohenfiles.com/jarvis-iv.pdf

35   Ezek. 43.1 and; 44.1–2.

36   Zollo, *Songwriters on Songwriting*.

37   Isa. 24.19, Ps. 98.5.

38   Ps. 98,8.

39   Bereshit Rabbah 20,12; Zohar Hadash, Bereshit.

40   For an alternative interpretation of *You Want It Darker* see Rabbi
     Lord Jonathan Sacks: https://www.youtube.com/watch?v=2s3
     kQSZ_Qxk

41   Leonard Cohen, *You Want It Darker*, album launch event at The
     Official Residence of Canada, Los Angeles, 13 October 2016;
     https://www.leonardcohenfiles.com/darkerlaunchevent.pdf.

42   Interview with David Remnick, *New Yorker*, 17 October 2016;
     https://www.youtube.com/watch?v=BVpG3tOonOQh-
     ttps://www.newyorker.com/magazine/2016/10/17/
     Cohen-cohen-makes-it-darker

Epilogue – A Modern-Day *Paytan*?

1   Author correspondence with John MacKenna, September 2020.

2   *Between Your Love and Mine: A Requiem by Leonard Cohen*, accessible
    at https://www.leonardcohenfiles.com/requiem2017.pdf. John
    MacKenna's profound and touching to tribute to Leonard Cohen,
    on the first anniversary of his death, can be heard at https://
    www.rte.ie/culture/2020/0408/1129295-listen-leonard-co-
    hen-remembered-by-his-friend-john-mackenna/

3   *Mishkan HaNefesh: Yom Kippur* (New York: CCAR Press, 2015),
    p. 207.

INDEX OF SONG TITLES

INDEX

A NOTE ON THE AUTHOR

Harry Freedman is Britain's leading author of popular works of Jewish culture and history. His publications include *The Talmud: A Biography; Kabbalah: Secrecy, Scandal and the Soul; The Murderous History of Bible Translations; Reason to Believe, The Gospels' Veiled Agenda* and *Britain's Jews: Confidence, Maturity, Anxiety*. You can follow his regular articles on harryfreedman.substack.com.

harryfreedmanbooks.com
@harryfreedman1

A NOTE ON THE TYPE

The text of this book is set in Perpetua. This typeface is an adaptation of a style of letter that had been popularised for monumental work in stone by Eric Gill. Large scale drawings by Gill were given to Charles Malin, a Parisian punch-cutter, and his hand-cut punches were the basis for the font issued by Monotype. First used in a private translation called 'The Passion of Perpetua and Felicity', the italic was originally called Felicity.